Engaging Islam

Biblical Answers to 10 Common Islamic Objections

Mitchell Beecher

Scripture quotations taken from the (NASB®) New American Standard Bible®, Copyright © 1960, 1971, 1977, 1995, 2020 by The Lockman Foundation. Used by permission. All rights reserved.
lockman.org

ISBN: 979-8-9910968-0-5 (Paperback)
ISBN: 979-8-9910968-1-2 (E-Book)
ISBN: 979-8-9910968-2-9 (Audible)

Library of Congress Control Number: 2024914916

Book design by Lou Designs.

First printing edition 2024.

www.timelesstruthcollection.com

Table of Contents

Preface

In a world where faith and beliefs often clash, dialogue awaits discovery. *Engaging Islam* is a journey of exploration. We sometimes find it hard to confront common objections with clarity and conviction. This book is not just an intellectual exercise but a heartfelt endeavor to bridge understanding and faith. It is to offer reasoned responses grounded in love and truth.

As a born-again Christian, I do not come to you as a seasoned theologian or a scholar with endless credentials. Instead, I come as someone who loves Jesus deeply. I have experienced His transformative power in my life. My passion is to share the truth about Him with others. Others who might hold misconceptions or doubts about the Christian faith. This book is born out of countless conversations, prayers, and a relentless desire to see others understand the hope and love found in Jesus Christ.

The purpose of this book is straightforward: to provide believers with informed responses to prevalent objections raised by our Muslim friends. Each chapter speaks to a distinct challenge. I offer a perspective grounded in both faith and reason. By understanding these objections and the context in which they arise, we can foster meaningful dialogues that bridge gaps and build relationships based on mutual respect and truth.

In this book, we will address ten fundamental objections. These objections range from the pervasive claim of the Bible's corruption to the complex doctrines of the Trinity and original sin. We will explore historical and textual evidence, analyze theological concepts, and provide practical insights for engaging in thoughtful and respectful conversations. Prepare for a journey of discovery, reflection, and enlightenment as we confront these objections with unwavering resolve and a heart full of love.

Although this book addresses ten distinct objections, the responses often intersect and resonate with each other. This is the beauty of the Bible - it weaves a single, cohesive story throughout its entirety. Also, you do not need to read this book in order. Feel free to jump to the objection you are interested in exploring. Think of it as a manual or a reference guide.

This journey is about answering objections and growing in our faith and understanding. It is about equipping ourselves to be better witnesses of Christ's love and truth in a world that desperately needs both. So, let us dive in together! Open your hearts and minds, and get ready to explore, learn, and share the incredible truth of Jesus Christ.

For His glory,
Mitchell Beecher

Introduction

Before answering the common objections, we must take a step back and look at the big picture. In this picture, we see God in the heavens and humanity below on the earth. There is a great chasm that separates God and humans. The divide between God and humanity is the central issue that causes friction between Christianity and Islam. How can we bridge this gap to have communion with God and share eternity with Him? Each faith offers its profound answer to this question, grounded in its unique theological beliefs and teachings.

The Christian Answer

Christianity provides a unique solution to bridging the separation between God and humans, rooted in the nature of God as love and the redemptive work of Jesus Christ. Christianity centers on one God, Yahweh, who exists in three persons: the Father, the Son (Jesus Christ), and the Holy Spirit. This triune God loves perfectly and is, in essence, love (agape). Humanity, created in the image of God, was designed to participate in this love. However, for love to be genuine, it must be voluntary. The tragic consequence of humanity's voluntary rejection (Fall of Man) of God is the rejection of love itself, which leads to spiritual death.

Sin in Christianity is not merely about committing wrong acts; it is fundamentally about rejecting the sustainer of life, Yahweh. This sin has devastated our souls and the world, creating an unbridgeable chasm between God and humanity. The problem is compounded by our inability to undo our sins or restore ourselves to God.

God, in His infinite love and mercy, initiated the restoration through Jesus Christ. Jesus, meaning "God saves," entered human history, not altering His divine nature but taking on human form. Born sinless, He lived a life of perfect obedience to God, embodying the life humans were meant to live. His ultimate mission was to die the death we deserve because of our sins.

Jesus claimed to be God and substantiated this claim by taking upon Himself the sin of the world. Through His death on the cross, He paid the penalty for sin, and His resurrection from the dead proved His authority as the Author of Life. By accepting Jesus' sacrifice, believers are transformed and granted eternal life. This acceptance involves repentance and faith in Jesus, who is "the way" to restored relationship with God.

The core message of Christianity is that humanity's fundamental problem is sin, and we are powerless to save ourselves. The good news (Gospel) is that God, in His love, provided a way of salvation through Jesus. This sacrificial act on the cross, confirmed by Jesus' resurrection, offers hope and transformation to all who repent and follow Him. The Holy Spirit works within believers to make them more like Christ, and they are called to share the Gospel to the ends of the earth.

In essence, Christianity proclaims that the bridge between God and humans is not built by human effort but by the divine intervention of Jesus Christ, who is "the way" to reconciliation and eternal life.

The Islamic Answer

Islam provides an entirely different answer to the question of how to bridge the separation between God and humans. The Islamic answer is grounded in the concept of submission to the will of Allah and adherence to divine guidance. Islam, meaning 'submission,' teaches that humans are to submit to the sovereignty of Allah, who predestined the universe and created mankind with the express purpose of worshipping Him (Quran 51:56). To guide humanity, Allah sent prophets (Quran 4:163-165), who exemplified submission to Allah and are thus considered Muslims, meaning those who submit. This includes followers of prophets even before Muhammad.

The prophets received divine scriptures dictated by angels, with each revelation tailored to the needs and capacities of the people at the time. These scriptures include the Torah and the Injeel (Gospels). However, over time, people did not faithfully follow these revelations. In response, Allah, in His mercy, sent Muhammad and the Quran, which is considered the final and perfect revelation (Quran 5:3). Islam views itself as the culmination of all world religions, and those who follow other religions are seen as either misled or rebellious.

In Islam, all people are held accountable for their sins, and no one can intercede on their behalf. Mankind is seen as inherently ignorant and in need of both *aqeed* (correct beliefs) and *sharia* (guidance on how to live). Following these is considered the right way to live.

Prophets in Islam hold a special status, higher than all other people, chosen by Allah to lead. The term 'prophet' in the Quran refers to a divinely appointed leader, not necessarily one who prophesies in the conventional sense, as seen in Christianity.

Sharia , derived from the Quran, exemplified in Muhammad's life, and explained by imams, is more than just Islamic law. It is seen as the solution to mankind's ignorance, guiding believers to a life of peace with Allah and abundant blessings. On the last day, those who have obeyed *sharia* and performed well *may* receive Allah's mercy and be granted entry into heaven, where eternal rewards and pleasures await.

Sharia means 'the way,' providing the framework for living a life following Allah's will and achieving ultimate reconciliation with Him.

In Summary

Both Christianity and Islam offer profound answers to the separation between God and humanity. Christianity emphasizes the redemptive work of Jesus Christ, who bridges the gap through His sacrificial death and resurrection. Islam focuses on submission to Allah and adherence to His guidance through the prophets and *sharia* . Understanding these perspectives provides a foundation for meaningful dialogue about faith and theology. Now, on to answering some common objections.

Chapter 1

The Bible is Corrupted

The Bible is often claimed to have been altered and thus unreliable. We will explore the historical and scholarly evidence that refutes this claim by demonstrating the meticulous preservation of biblical texts throughout history.

We will examine ancient manuscripts like the *Codex Vaticanus* and *Codex Sinaiticus* . Additionally, the role of the *Masoretic Text* and its careful transmission process shows that accuracy has been maintained over centuries. We will see that there is a wealth of New Testament manuscripts available for comparison. Many of these manuscripts date back as early as the 2nd century. Additionally, archeological discoveries such as the *Dead Sea Scrolls* and various inscriptions provide external corroboration. These discoveries align with the biblical narratives and reinforce the text's historical authenticity.

Biblical Reliability - Document Evidence

The *Codex Vaticanus* and *Codex Sinaiticus* are two of the oldest known complete manuscripts of the Bible. Both date back to the 4th century and show remarkable consistency with each other and later manuscripts. This consistency highlights that today's biblical texts have been accurately transmitted over the centuries.

Another critical piece of evidence comes from the *Masoretic Text* . The *Masoretic Text* is the authoritative Hebrew text of the Jewish Bible. The Masoretes, a group of Jewish scribes active between the 7th and 10th centuries, developed an extensive system of checks and balances to ensure the accurate copying of scriptures. They meticulously counted every letter, word, and verse in their copied manuscripts. This process vastly reduces the possibility of errors and alterations over time.

Additionally, the discovery of thousands of New Testament manuscripts, some dating as early as the 2nd century, adds further weight to the reliability of biblical transmission. These early copies, which include papyri fragments like P52 (the John Rylands Fragment), contain text that closely matches later versions. These manuscripts confirm the textual stability of the New Testament over nearly two millennia.

The *Dead Sea Scrolls* provide a detailed analysis validating the accuracy of biblical transmission. Discovered in the mid-20th century, these ancient texts date from around the 3rd century BC to the 1st century AD. The scrolls contain portions of every book of the Hebrew Bible (except Esther) and demonstrate minimal variance from the traditional *Masoretic Text* . For instance, the Great Isaiah Scroll is nearly identical to the Masoretic version. Once again, we have strong indications of significant continuity in the transmission process over a thousand years.

The Septuagint, an ancient Greek translation of the Hebrew Scriptures, offers further proof of textual accuracy. While some differences are due to translation nuances, the consistency between the Septuagint and later Hebrew texts reinforces the notion of careful preservation practices among ancient scribes.

Numerous manuscript discoveries affirm the reliability of the New Testament. Despite some minor differences, codices such as Alexandrinus and Ephraemi Rescriptus largely corroborate the content found in earlier manuscripts.

Biblical Reliability - Archeological Evidence

Archeological findings offer additional support for biblical accounts and the integrity of manuscripts. Inscriptions and artifacts discovered in ancient sites like Jericho and Jerusalem align with biblical narratives. For example, the Tel Dan Stele references the *House of David* . This corroborates biblical accounts of King David's dynasty.

The *Pool of Siloam* , uncovered in 2004, aligns with references in the Gospel of John, where Jesus heals a blind man (John 9:1-11). Such discoveries lend credibility to the geographical and historical context of the biblical stories and support their authenticity.

Inscriptions like the Pontius Pilate Stone, discovered in Caesarea Maritima, confirm the historical presence of figures mentioned in the New Testament. This artifact contains inscriptions mentioning Pilate, the Roman governor who ordered Jesus' crucifixion, cited in all four Gospels.

Lastly, ongoing archeological digs continue to uncover artifacts that match biblical descriptions. Modern discoveries continue to strengthen the argument for the Bible's historical reliability. For example, the recent unearthing of extensive fortifications at Khirbet Qeiyafa supports the biblical account of fortified cities in Judah during King David's reign.

These historical evidence collectively illustrate the rigorous transmission processes, archeological consistency, and scholarly validation. From the document and archeological evidence alone, we have complete confidence that the Bible is accurate, reliable, and has not been changed.

Internal Consistency of Biblical Manuscripts

One of the most compelling evidence for the Bible is its internal consistency. Despite being written by 40 authors over 1500 years, the Bible presents a unified narrative of God's character and redemptive plan. Though different in many aspects, the Old and New Testaments work together seamlessly to tell the story of humanity's creation, fall, redemption, and final restoration with God. This harmony is not merely superficial; it reinforces profound theological themes that are remarkably consistent throughout the Bible.

Various authors across different periods convey a cohesive image of God's character. For example, Moses, David, Isaiah, and Paul all describe God as just and merciful, slow to anger, and abounding in steadfast love. This unifying depiction appears despite these writers' distinct historical contexts and personal experiences. The coherence suggests that the authors were inspired by a single divine source - which Paul writes to Timothy in 2 Timothy 3:16.

The narrative unity is also reflected in how biblical authors address the concept of salvation. Throughout the Bible, salvation is depicted as a divine act initiated by God out of His love for humanity. From the sacrifices in the Old Testament to the sacrificial death of Jesus in the New Testament, the theme remains consistent: humanity's relationship with God is restored through grace and sacrifice. We will explore this concept in later chapters - specifically Chapter 8.

Consistencies are also found in prophetic books like Isaiah (Chapters 9, 52, and 53) and Micah (Chapter 5). These books contain numerous predictions about the life of a Messiah. Over 300 prophecies are fulfilled in the New Testament through the life and work of Jesus Christ. These prophecies, written hundreds of years before Christ, align closely with New Testament narratives.

Looking at significant themes such as justice, mercy, and righteousness are prevalent throughout the Scriptures. Micah 6:8 emphasizes walking humbly with God and doing justice. James 1:27 echoes similar sentiments about pure and undefiled religion. This thematic resonance across different books and genres points to the internal consistency of the Bible. It suggests a comprehensive, integrated message that transcends individual contributions. Once again, this points to divine inspiration.

Historical accounts in books like Kings and Chronicles provide a framework for understanding Israel's history. Wisdom literature such as Proverbs and Ecclesiastes offers moral guidance and reflections on human existence. These genres create a rich tapestry that enhances our comprehension of biblical teachings.

Poetic books like Psalms capture the emotional and spiritual dimensions of faith. For example, Psalm 51, a plea for mercy after David's sin with Bathsheba, complements the narrative account in 2 Samuel 11-12. In the same way, prophetic books often revisit themes introduced in the historical narratives (e.g., calls for repentance and promises of future hope). This interdependence among genres strengthens the Bible's unity, and each book support its reliability.

The New Testament letters frequently reference Old Testament passages to validate theological points. Paul's writings, particularly Romans and Galatians, draw extensively from Old Testament scripture to explain concepts like justification by faith (see Chapter 8). Hebrews elaborates on how the Old Covenant foreshadowed the New Covenant established through Jesus Christ. These cross-references demonstrate how different parts of the Bible interact cohesively.

Biblical principles transcend cultural and historical contexts which makes the Bible timeless. Commands like love your neighbor (Leviticus 19:18) and seeking justice and mercy (Micah 6:8) remain pertinent regardless of time period or social setting. These principles are reiterated in the New Testament. Jesus' teachings about ethical living, including the *Sermon on the Mount* (Matthew 5-7), resonate with Christians across generations and cultures.

Moral and ethical principles found in the Bible apply universally. These principles were not only for the original audiences. The principle of love your enemy (Matthew 5:44) challenges modern societal norms. Biblical principles like humility, forgiveness, and charity continue to guide individuals in all societies.

Concepts of compassion, justice, and stewardship are deeply rooted in biblical texts. These concepts resonate with broader human values. By surpassing specific cultural and historical settings, the Bible provides a common ethical ground for dialogue between Christians and Muslims.

Internal consistency, a uniform message over centuries, prophecies of Jesus long before his birth, detailed descriptions of Jesus' death before the Romans invented crucifixion, and timeless Biblical principles (both moral and ethical) that have penetrated societies for centuries can give us total reassurance that the Bible is not corrupted.

Biblical Manuscripts and Other Ancient Texts

Comparing the manuscript preservation of the Bible with other ancient texts offers substantial evidence supporting its reliability. A quantitative comparison reveals that the New Testament stands out due to the sheer number of available manuscripts. With over 5,600 Greek manuscripts, 10,000 Latin manuscripts, and 9,300 others in various languages, the total exceeds 24,000 (Slick, M., 2008). In contrast, works like Plato's *Tetralogies* have only seven extant copies. Aristotle's works have about 49. This abundance allows for cross-referencing and accounts for greater accuracy among the biblical manuscripts than other ancient texts.

When examining the time span between the original writings and their earliest copies, the New Testament again emerges favorably. The gap is approximately 50-100 years. For most ancient texts, such as those by Herodotus or Thucydides, the span extends to 1,300 years. Homer's *Iliad* has a gap of around 500 years with about 643 copies available. The Quran has around 60 fragments, totaling roughly 4000 pages. These pages date to around 168 years after Muhammad's death. Nonetheless, the shorter period for the New Testament significantly reduces the potential for textual corruption - increasing its credibility and reliability as a historical document.

The consistency among New Testament manuscripts is remarkable. Textual scholars indicate that the New Testament documents maintain a 99.5% textual purity. The .5% variant mainly involves minor spelling differences or word order changes (Slick, M., 2008). Such a high degree of accuracy is unparalleled among other ancient manuscripts.

Historical and archeological findings are crucial in affirming the events and characters described in the Bible. Numerous discoveries correlate with biblical narratives. An example would be the *Dead Sea Scrolls* found in the mid-20th century. These scrolls contain portions of the Old Testament dating back to the 1st Century BC. These scrolls closely match later manuscripts, demonstrating biblical texts' remarkable consistency and preservation over centuries

(Manuscript Support for the Bible's Relia. Reasoning From The S., n.d.).

Archeological discoveries also substantiate specific biblical accounts. The excavation of Jericho aligns with the biblical description of its destruction. Similarly, inscriptions referencing King David and Pontius Pilate validate the historical existence of these figures mentioned in the Bible. These external findings support the narrative integrity and historical reliability of the biblical texts.

There are a few ancient non-biblical texts referencing biblical events and figures to consider. The writings of Flavius Josephus, a first-century Jewish historian, mention Jesus, John the Baptist, and James. Such external sources reinforce the idea that biblical events are not merely myths but are rooted in historical facts. We will review these external sources in Chapter 6 when discussing Jesus' crucifixion.

Norman Geisler and Bruce Metzger are renowned textual critics and historians. Their work strongly supports the reliability of the New Testament texts based on extensive manuscript evidence. According to Geisler, no other ancient work has as much documentary support, both in quantity and the proximity of manuscripts to the original writers (Slick, M., 2008).

Bruce Metzger's research highlights the minimal impact of textual variants on the New Testament's core message. Despite numerous minor differences, these variants do not affect any essential Christian doctrine or moral commandment. This consensus among scholars boosts biblical manuscripts' textual integrity and reliability.

Muslims often argue that Christians have intentionally manipulated or added statements to fit the Christian narrative. Scholars address this, too. Textual criticism methods, which involve comparing various manuscript copies, reveal that significant intentional alterations are virtually nonexistent. Instead, the variations found are typical of any ancient document subject to manual copying processes over centuries.

The preservation methods of biblical manuscripts set them apart from other ancient texts. The meticulous scribe traditions observed by Jewish communities ensured the careful copying of Old Testament texts. Scribes took extreme measures, such as counting letters and words, to prevent errors. This dedication to accuracy is evident in the consistency observed among ancient Hebrew manuscripts discovered at Qumran and those used centuries later.

The longevity and accuracy of biblical manuscripts can be attributed to their abundant copies and the meticulous scribal practices. The relatively short time gap between the original compositions and the earliest surviving copies further minimizes the risk of textual deviations. As a result, the Bible stands as a uniquely well-preserved ancient document.

Textual Criticism Arguments

As stated above, Muslims often assert that early church leaders made deliberate changes to biblical texts to align more closely with evolving theological doctrines. However, historical evidence and scholarly research debunk these claims. Many of the alleged modifications need more manuscript evidence, which indicates they are more speculative than factual.

Historical scrutiny reveals that some scribes did make errors - such as spelling mistakes or repeated lines. These were unintentional. The sheer number of manuscripts available for comparison today makes it relatively straightforward for scholars to identify and correct these mistakes. Some accused alterations appear in only a few manuscripts and are not representative of the broader textual tradition - undermining the argument that intentional changes had any widespread impact (Inspiration, Preservation, and New Testament Textual Criticism | Bible.org).

Another focus of criticism is textual variants. The existence of variants does not negate the accuracy of biblical transmission. Variants are common in all ancient texts due to the manual copying process, and the New Testament is no exception. The vast majority of textual variants are minor, such as differences in spelling or word order, which do not significantly affect the text's meaning.

Significant theological doctrines, like the divinity of Christ, the resurrection, and salvation, are consistently affirmed across diverse manuscripts. Scholars estimate that only a tiny fraction of the text, less than 1%, contains any meaningful variation. These differences are acknowledged and discussed openly, which provides transparency and strengthens the reliability of the text. The rigorous work of textual critics ensures that the original wording can be reconstructed accurately (Textual Reliability of the New Testament. www.tektonics.org).

Explaining the principles of textual criticism and how they affirm the accuracy of biblical transmission is essential for understanding why the Bible is reliable despite these criticisms. Textual criticism involves comparing thousands of existing manuscripts to ascertain the most likely original text. Scholars consider factors such as the manuscript's age, geographical distribution, and internal coherence in their evaluations.

For example, earlier manuscripts are more reliable because they are closer in time to the original writings. When a reading is found in manuscripts from diverse geographical locations, it suggests authenticity due to its widespread acceptance. Textual critics also employ linguistic and literary analysis to detect and correct later insertions or modifications.

This scientific approach to studying ancient texts has confirmed the reliability of the biblical manuscripts to a high degree of certainty. By reconstructing the original text through careful and systematic comparison of available manuscripts, textual criticism plays a crucial role in maintaining the integrity of the Bible. It provides a sound methodology that reassures believers in the trustworthiness of the scriptures they read today (Inspiration, Preservation, and New Testament Textual Criticism | Bible.org).

Summary

When faced with objections regarding the reliability of biblical texts, it's helpful to highlight the robust manuscript evidence available for the New Testament. With over 24,000 manuscripts, complete and fragmented, the New Testament stands unparalleled in its documentary support compared to other ancient texts.

Textual criticism has achieved near-complete accuracy in reconstructing the New Testament - dismantling arguments on supposed widespread corruption. Scholars agree that the remaining areas of uncertainty are minuscule and do not impact critical teachings. It's important to frame this within the context of how other ancient texts are treated. Historians often accept the reliability of texts with far fewer manuscripts and far more significant time gaps between original composition and existing copies.

Looking at ancient manuscripts like the *Codex Vaticanus* and the *Codex Sinaiticus* and considering the meticulous scribe practices of the Masoretes, we have seen how carefully biblical texts have been preserved over time. The consistency found in New Testament manuscripts, some of which date back to the 2nd century, further reinforces the idea that these texts have been faithfully transmitted through generations.

The *Dead Sea Scrolls* provide compelling evidence against the objection that the Bible has been corrupted or altered. The remarkable alignment between these ancient texts and later versions strengthens the continuity and trustworthiness of biblical documents.

Even with all of this, many Muslims will still argue the textual variants and allegations of intentional modifications. While it is true that variations exist among manuscripts, the vast majority are minor and do not affect the core messages or doctrines of Christianity. Rigorous textual criticism methods allow scholars to reconstruct original texts accurately and ensure the essential Christian teachings remain intact.

The documented preservation of biblical texts affirms their historical reliability and fortifies Christians' confidence in the scriptures.

The journey toward proving the Bible's reliability does not end here. Ongoing archeological discoveries and advancements in textual studies continue to reinforce the evidence for biblical credibility. As we move forward, let us remain open to learning and exploring, grounded in the knowledge that our scriptures have stood the test of time.

Reflection

How does the detailed manuscript evidence presented in the chapter affect your view of the Bible's reliability and authenticity?

What are your thoughts on the significance of the *Codex Vaticanus* and *Codex Sinaiticus* in establishing the Bible's textual consistency over the centuries?

How do the meticulous practices of the Masoretes in preserving the Hebrew Bible influence your confidence in the accuracy of the Old Testament?

Considering the discovery of the *Dead Sea Scrolls* , how do these findings impact the argument against the corruption of the Bible?

How does the sheer number of New Testament manuscripts and the relatively short time span between the originals and earliest copies contribute to the argument for the Bible's reliability?

What role do you believe archeological findings, such as the Tel Dan Stele and the Pool of Siloam, play in supporting the historical credibility of the Bible?

How do the Bible's internal consistency and unified narrative, despite being written by multiple authors over many centuries, affect your understanding of its divine inspiration?

What are your reflections on comparing the preservation of biblical manuscripts to that of other ancient texts, such as those of Plato or Aristotle?

How does the discussion on textual criticism and the high degree of accuracy in reconstructing the original New Testament text influence your view on alleged intentional alterations of the Bible?

What are your thoughts on the ongoing relevance and application of biblical principles, such as love, justice, and humility, in today's world and the context of interfaith dialogue between Christians and Muslims?

Chapter 2

There are Many Different Bibles and Versions

The existence of many different Bibles and versions highlights the rich tapestry of scriptural interpretation and translation efforts over centuries. Understanding why these many translations came into being is vital to appreciating their unique roles and audiences. Each version, from the venerable King James Version (KJV) to the more contemporary New International Version (NIV), offers distinct linguistic and stylistic features tailored to the needs of diverse readerships. Each of these served different purposes and catered to varied readerships over time. We will explore the core reasons for these variations and how different translations address the historical, cultural, and linguistic contexts in which they were produced.

Foundational Differences in Bible Translations

Understanding the multitude of Bible translations and their foundational differences is crucial for addressing diverse audiences. One can start by looking at major translations such as the King James Version (KJV), New International Version (NIV), and English Standard Version (ESV). Each of these translations serves different purposes and caters to varied readerships. For instance, the KJV, first published in 1611, is revered for its majestic language and historical influence. It primarily targets readers who appreciate literary classicism and a more formalized version of biblical text. In contrast, the NIV, completed in 1978, aims to balance readability and accuracy, making it suitable for a modern audience seeking clarity in everyday language. The ESV, published in 2001, tends toward a more literal translation while maintaining readability - appealing to those who desire an accurate yet comprehensible text.

The historical contexts behind these translations have significantly influenced reader comprehension. The KJV emerged when English literature and language flourished and incorporated the Renaissance's linguistic richness. This context has made the KJV enduringly popular among traditionalist readers and those in liturgical settings. On the other hand, the NIV was developed post-World War II. During this period, there was a growing demand for accessible religious texts that the general public could easily understand without a scholarly background. The ESV came about in response to a mid-20th century trend towards meticulous study Bibles. These study Bibles emphasized precise adherence to original manuscripts while being accessible to contemporary readers. These historical backgrounds show how each translation aimed to meet the needs of its time, enhancing or challenging reader comprehension depending on the era's literacy levels and cultural dynamics.

Language nuances and cultural contexts play essential roles in translation accuracy. Translators must navigate differences in grammatical structures, idiomatic expressions, and cultural references between the source languages (Hebrew, Aramaic, Greek) and the target language (English). For example, Hebrew poetry relies heavily on parallelism and wordplay - a challenge to replicate in English without losing some meanings or rhythms. A Hebrew word like ' *chesed* ,' which encompasses mercy, kindness, and loyalty, may not have a direct English equivalent. Additionally, cultural contexts, such as ancient Near Eastern customs versus modern Western practices, necessitate careful consideration to preserve the original intent and essence of the message. These nuances make translation an art as much as a science.

Comparing readability versus literal accuracy is another vital aspect of Bible translations. Like the ESV, Literal translations strive to remain as close to the original text as possible - both sentence structure and specific wording. This approach provides a high level of fidelity to the original manuscripts. Still, it can sometimes result in less fluid reading for contemporary audiences—conversely, versions like the NIV aim for dynamic equivalence. Dynamic equivalence prioritizes thought-for-thought translation over word-for-word accuracy. This method enhances readability and ensures the text resonates with modern readers but may introduce interpretative biases or lose some nuances of the original language. Depending on whether one values textual precision or ease of understanding more highly, both approaches have their merits.

To dive into the importance of translation philosophy, it is essential to consider the principles behind literal versus dynamic translations and their implications. Literal translations, such as the KJV and ESV, focus on maintaining the exact form and structure of the original languages. This philosophy is rooted in the belief that every word in the scripture is inspired and carries significant meaning. As a result, these translations often provide a richer, more nuanced understanding of the biblical text. This is highly valuable for in-depth study and explanation. However, the literal approach can sometimes lead to awkward phrasing and complex sentences. Some might find this a hindrance and hard to comprehend.

The thought-for-thought approach (e.g., NIV) aims to convey ideas and concepts in a way that is easily understood. This philosophy acknowledges that language and culture evolve, and thus, the message of the Bible should be communicated in a way that resonates with modern audiences. These translations are more readable and accessible - ideal for devotional reading and outreach ministries. Literal translations (e.g., NASB, KJV) are particularly beneficial in academic and theological settings. These versions facilitate rigorous analysis and deeper exploration of biblical themes and doctrines.

The thought-for-thought approach can sometimes lead to interpretative liberties. Translators potentially inject their theological biases into the text. Balancing these philosophies requires discernment and understanding the translation's intended purpose.

Discrepancies Between Various Bible Versions

Addressing discrepancies that may arise between various Bible versions and providing strategies for reconciling them is crucial for Christians to deepen their faith and engage with Muslims. One of the first steps in this journey is identifying common inconsistencies across translations and understanding the underlying reasons behind these variations. Many differences in Bible translations can be attributed to translators' choices regarding language, cultural context, and the textual sources they use.

Inconsistencies may also arise from the different ancient manuscripts used as base texts. The King James Version primarily relies on the *Textus Receptus* . Modern translations like the New International Version often use a broader range of earlier sources, such as the *Dead Sea Scrolls* and *Codex Vaticanus* . These older manuscripts can sometimes provide more accurate readings but may differ slightly from later texts.

Understanding the translator's purpose and theological perspective is critical to recognizing why some translations include or exclude specific phrases or words. Translators may incorporate or omit certain renderings based on denominational beliefs or interpretive traditions. This is evident in passages where doctrinally sensitive terms are translated in ways that align with particular theological views.

Investigating textual variations stemming from translation decisions and manuscript differences provides further insight into why these inconsistencies occur. As mentioned, translation decisions are influenced by linguistic complexities, cultural nuances, and historical contexts. Hebrew and Greek, the original languages of the Bible, have idiomatic expressions that may not have direct equivalents in English. Translators must decide whether to translate these idioms literally or adapt them to convey the intended meaning more clearly to modern readers.

A common objection Muslims raise is the ending of the Gospel of Mark. Some early manuscripts do not include

Mark 16:9-20. This discrepancy leads to variations in how different Bible versions handle these verses. Scholarly debate continues over which tradition represents the original text.

Techniques for harmonizing divergent passages among different versions become essential to address these variations (and to help guide conversations with Muslims). One effective method is parallel reading, which involves comparing multiple Bible versions side-by-side. This approach helps to see how different translations handle specific verses and provides a broader understanding of the text's possible meanings.

Another technique is simply engaging in group Bible studies. Discussing interpretations with others allows for collective wisdom and shared insights. Other believers can bring different translations and share how each version expresses a passage.

No matter the technique, the key is to ensure consistent core messages despite varying textual interpretations. The central themes of Christianity, such as the life, death, and resurrection of Jesus Christ, remain intact across all reputable translations. While wordings may differ, the fundamental doctrines and moral teachings are consistently conveyed. When responding to Muslim objections, focus on these core messages rather than getting overly concerned with minor textual differences.

Finally, maintaining a humble and open attitude toward scripture is beneficial. Recognizing that no single translation is perfect encourages continuous learning and exploration. Different versions can complement each other, enriching your faith journey and providing a more comprehensive picture of God's word. Reflecting on the Bible's overarching story from creation to redemption reinforces a unified understanding of its message.

Meticulous Process of Canonization

Within this argument, Muslims often address the different Bibles used by different Christian denominations. Canonization has been central to preserving the integrity of biblical texts. This journey began in ancient times when the writings that now comprise the Bible were first penned. Understanding how these texts were selected as authoritative requires examining the historical development and criteria used for their inclusion. From guidelines rooted in spiritual leadership to authentic consistency with existing divine revelations, each book had to meet rigorous standards.

The Old Testament books were initially recognized based on their use and acceptance within Jewish communities. Prophetic authority and divine inspiration were critical factors. For example, writings attributed to Moses, the prophets, or kings held significant weight. Over time, the collection was refined through communal practices and teachings, ensuring only those books deemed genuinely inspired made it into the canonical fold.

As Christianity emerged, early church leaders followed similar stringent processes for the New Testament. Apostolic authority played a crucial role; books needed to be connected directly to Jesus' apostles or their immediate followers. The authenticity and consistency of the message with the broader Christian faith were paramount in helping to maintain doctrinal purity across diverse congregations.

Early church councils were instrumental in formalizing the canon. These gatherings of Christian leaders sought to identify rather than decide the divinely inspired texts. Notable councils include Nicaea, Jamnia, and Carthage. The Council of Jamnia around 90 AD helped solidify the Hebrew Bible. Later councils like Carthage in 397 AD confirmed the 27 books of the New Testament we acknowledge today. These decisions reflected extensive debate, study, and prayerful consideration among respected theologians.

These councils were forums for discussing and addressing lingering disputes over specific texts. For instance, some debated the inclusion of books like Hebrews or Revelation. Yet, through collective discernment and adherence to established criteria—such as prophetic witness, widespread usage, and theological coherence—the councils achieved a firm consensus.

This communal recognition was an organizational measure and a profound testament to the collaborative effort to preserve sacred scripture's integrity. By gathering knowledge and negotiating understanding, the early Christians ensured that what was handed down reflected God's word.

The transmission and preservation of biblical manuscripts over centuries further illustrate the meticulous efforts to safeguard textual accuracy from the council meetings. Before printing technology, scribes painstakingly copied texts by hand. Each copy required enormous attention to detail to prevent errors. This process was vital for the Old and New Testaments, as initial inscriptions were on materials like papyrus, parchment, and stone.

In Chapter One, we reviewed how they were obsessively dedicated to preserving the original text. They developed a sophisticated system to ensure precision, including counting letters and words within manuscripts to verify accuracy. Also, individual letters could only be written after first checking the original text. Discoveries like the *Dead Sea Scrolls* , dating back to the 1st Century BC, have validated the *Masoretic Text's* reliability and showed minimal discrepancy over centuries of transmission.

Greek manuscripts from the first few centuries offer remarkable testimony to the preservation process for the New Testament. Textual fragments dated as early as AD 120 reveal close correspondence with later complete manuscripts. Scholars attribute this accuracy to the sheer number of surviving copies, which allows comprehensive cross-referencing and error correction. With thousands of manuscripts available, modern translations benefit from unparalleled textual scrutiny. Such detailed methodologies helped avoid mistakes and safeguarded the holy scriptures' sanctity.

Cross-Cultural Implications of Bible Translations

Cross-cultural translations of the Bible have played a significant role in promoting a global understanding of Christian teachings. Translators bridge linguistic and cultural gaps by translating the Bible into various languages and dialects, making the scripture accessible to a broader audience. This not only helps individuals understand biblical texts in their native languages but also fosters inclusivity within the Christian faith. The Word of God is for all people to have the opportunity to hear the Good News!

One prominent example of this bridging process is the work done in regions where multiple languages are spoken. Translators often have to navigate intricate linguistic differences to ensure that the translated text remains true to the original meaning while being understandable to the local people. This task requires a deep understanding of the source, target languages, and the cultural nuances that might affect interpretation (How Our Cultural Context Impacts the Way We Interpret Scripture | Faithward.org., 2022).

Localized translations are crucial for effective communication within diverse societies. Translating the Bible into a local language makes it more relatable and easier for the community to understand. This practice respects the people's cultural heritage and identity and helps make the biblical teachings more relevant to their daily lives and cultural practices.

A great example is in African countries where numerous ethnic groups and languages are present. The impact of localized translations has been profound! Communities with limited or no access to the Bible in their mother tongue can now engage more personally and meaningfully with the scripture. This fosters a sense of belonging within the Christian community and promotes spiritual growth as individuals can meditate on and internalize the teachings without linguistic obstacles (webmaster, 2022).

However, maintaining theological accuracy while adapting to different cultural contexts presents several challenges. Translators must ensure that the core messages remain intact despite the variations in language structures and expressions. Adaptations include using familiar idioms or metaphors that resonate with culture while conveying the same theological concepts in the original text. Yet, it's essential to avoid distortions that could lead to misunderstandings or misinterpretations of key doctrines.

Translators need to be well-versed in theological principles and the socio-cultural background of the community to navigate these challenges effectively.

Summary

We have examined the key reasons behind many Bible translations and versions. We highlighted the foundational differences among major translations like the King James Version (KJV), New International Version (NIV), and English Standard Version (ESV). Each translation was shaped by distinct historical contexts, catering to different readerships with unique needs.

The KJV, rooted in the linguistic richness of the Renaissance, has maintained its appeal among those who appreciate its formal language and historical significance. The NIV emerged post-World War II, designed for accessibility and modern readability, while the ESV straddles the line between literal accuracy and comprehensibility.

A critical comparison of readability versus literal accuracy helped highlight the pros and cons of different translation philosophies. While literal translations like the ESV adhere closely to original texts, they may pose readability issues. Though they risk introducing interpretative biases, dynamic translations like the NIV prioritize clarity and ease of understanding.

We explored translators' challenges - linguistic structures, idiomatic expressions, and cultural contexts that influence translation accuracy. Translators must ensure that crucial concepts are faithfully rendered without losing meaning or rhythm.

Discrepancies between various Bible versions underscored the importance of recognizing common inconsistencies and their origins. Variations arise from translation choices, manuscript sources, and theological perspectives. Identifying these differences is vital for deeper theological engagement and discussions with our Muslim friends.

Despite the textual variations, core Christian messages remain consistent, emphasizing Jesus Christ's life, death, and resurrection.

The meticulous canonization process revealed how early church leaders preserved the integrity of biblical texts through rigorous criteria and communal practices. Old and New Testament books were selected based on prophetic authority, apostolic connections, and doctrinal consistency. Early church councils played significant roles in formalizing the canon and ensured that only genuinely inspired texts were included.

Lastly, we discussed the cross-cultural implications of Bible translations. We emphasized how localized translations promote inclusivity and spiritual growth within diverse communities. Translators must balance theological accuracy with cultural relevance, navigating linguistic and cultural nuances to effectively convey the Bible's message.

It becomes clear that understanding the multitude of Bible translations involves appreciating the historical, linguistic, and cultural intricacies that shape them. Critically evaluating these elements helps us with our evangelistic efforts toward Muslims. Ultimately, the goal remains to deepen one's faith and engage thoughtfully in discussions about Christianity.

Reflection

How do the various Bible translations, such as the NASB, KJV, NIV, and ESV, enhance or challenge your understanding of biblical texts and their relevance today?

How do you balance the importance of literal accuracy versus readability in your personal Bible study and devotional practices?

How does understanding translators' challenges, such as dealing with idiomatic expressions and cultural contexts, affect your appreciation of different Bible versions?

What strategies do you find effective for reconciling discrepancies between Bible translations when discussing with others, especially those of different faiths like Islam?

How does the process of canonization and the criteria used to select biblical texts influence your confidence in the Bible's authority and authenticity?

How do cross-cultural translations of the Bible and the efforts to make scripture accessible to diverse communities affect your view on the universality of the Christian message?

In what ways do you see the differences in translation philosophies (literal vs. dynamic) affecting the interpretation and application of biblical principles in contemporary Christian life?

How do you approach conversations about the reliability and consistency of the Bible when engaging with Muslim friends who raise objections based on textual variations?

Chapter 3

Jesus is Not God and Never Claimed to Be

Examining whether Jesus claimed to be God is a pivotal subject in Christian theology and is often brought up by Muslims. We will scrutinize specific biblical passages where Jesus' statements are interpreted as affirmations of His divinity. My goal is to provide a thorough analysis based on the texts from the New Testament, particularly the Gospel of John, and how these statements align with the theological understanding of Jesus within Christianity.

We will explore some of Jesus' key declarations in the Gospels, such as His use of "I am" and other self-referential terms that parallel Old Testament references to Yahweh. We will also discuss how these statements were perceived by His contemporaries, especially considering the reactions of Jewish leaders who accused Him of blasphemy. We will look at Jesus' claim of unity with the Father, the Greek terminology used, and its implications for the concept of the Trinity.

Jesus' Explicit Statements About His Divinity

In the Gospel of John, Jesus makes several declarations that explicitly affirm His divinity. One such statement is found in John 8:58, where Jesus declares, "Before Abraham was born, I am." The Greek word for "I am" is " *egō eimi* ". This proclamation is profound because it directly echoes God's self-identification to Moses in Exodus 3:14, where God says to Moses, "I AM WHO I AM." By using this phrase, Jesus not only implies His pre-existence but also aligns Himself with the eternal, self-existing nature of God. The significance of this claim is undeniable and demonstrates Jesus' assertion of His divine identity.

This statement would have been particularly shocking to His contemporaries. The Jewish audience understood the use of "I am" without a predicate, and in Greek, "Ego Eimi" refers to Yahweh. The audience's reaction in John 8:59, where they pick up stones to throw at Him, underscores their understanding of the theological implications of His words. They perceived it as blasphemy because Jesus was equating Himself with God. This alone was an act punishable by death under Jewish law. This reaction highlights the gravity of Jesus' declaration and reinforces the perception of His claim to divinity.

"I am" signifies more than just existence; it reflects a continuous presence and involvement in the unfolding history of salvation. In Christian theology, Jesus' identification with "I AM" indicates His eternal existence and participation in God's redemptive plan. This declaration confirms Jesus' divine nature and His role within the Trinity. It gives prominence to His unique position as both God and man, eternally present, and active in the lives of believers.

In examining how Jesus' use of "I AM" aligns with God's self-identification in Exodus 3:14, we need to understand the significance of this phrase within the Jewish context. In Exodus, when Moses asks God for His name, God responds, "I AM WHO I AM." This is a declaration of His eternal, unchangeable, and self-existent nature. This name, Yahweh, became the most sacred and revered name for God among the Israelites as it signifies His unique and unparalleled divinity.

By using "I AM," Jesus deliberately connects Himself to this divine name. He identifies Himself with the God of Israel. This alignment is not a casual appropriation of a common phrase but a deliberate theological statement. It situates Jesus' ministry within the broader narrative of God's revelation and covenantal history with Israel. Jesus uses this divine self-referential term multiple times throughout the Gospel of John. Each time, He is reinforcing His divine identity and eternal nature.

The repeated use of "I AM" statements, such as "I am the bread of life" (John 6:35) and "I am the way, the truth, and the life" (John 14:6), consistently point to Jesus as the source of spiritual sustenance, guidance, and truth. These declarations are central to understanding Jesus' mission and identity as God incarnate. This directly links the Old Testament revelation of God and the New Testament fulfillment in Christ.

Another striking proclamation of Jesus' divinity is in John 10:30, where He states, "I and the Father are one." This declaration goes beyond mere unity of purpose or mission. The Greek word used here for "one" is "hen" (ν). "Hen" denotes essence or nature rather than agreement or relationship. By claiming oneness with the Father, Jesus asserts that He shares the same divine essence as God. This, too, reinforces His identity as part of the Trinity.

Once again, the immediate reaction of the Jewish leaders further emphasizes the weight of this claim. They accuse Him of blasphemy and attempt to stone Him (John 10:31-33), asserting that "You, being a man, make Yourself *out to be* God." This response highlights their understanding that Jesus was not merely speaking metaphorically about being united with God in spirit or mission but was making a profound theological assertion about His divine nature. Their reaction reveals that Jesus' audience recognized His statements as claims to deity - which directly challenged their monotheistic beliefs.

This proclamation also has deep implications for Christian doctrine. It serves as a foundational text for understanding the Trinity and illustrates the intimate and ontological unity between the Father and the Son. It affirms that Jesus is fully God, possessing the same divine attributes and authority as the Father.

Understanding the cultural context of Jesus' audience is crucial to grasp the radical nature of His claims fully. Jesus spoke to a predominantly Jewish audience deeply rooted in monotheistic traditions. The core of Jewish belief, encapsulated in the *Shema* (Deuteronomy 6:4), is the oneness of God: ""Hear, Israel! The Lord is our God, the

Lord is one!" Any claim to divinity by a human being would be seen as a direct challenge to this foundational belief.

In this context, Jesus' assertions of His divine nature were revolutionary and confrontational. His audience would have understood Him as challenging the prevailing interpretations of monotheism. Instead of introducing a new deity, Jesus revealed a more complex understanding of God's nature. A nature that includes the coexistence of the Father and the Son within the unified Godhead. This understanding would eventually be recognized and formalized in the doctrine of the Trinity.

Jesus' claims must also be viewed against first-century Jewish expectations of the Messiah. Many Jews awaited a political and military leader who would liberate them from Roman rule and restore the kingdom of Israel. In contrast, Jesus presented a different vision—one where the Messiah is not only a king but also divine, sharing in the very essence of God. This reinterpretation of messianic expectations redefined the relationship between humanity and God in a profound and transformative way.

Jesus - The 'Son of God'

In Chapter Four, we will discuss and go into more detail around the 'Son of God', but it is worth discussing here as part of this common objection.

The title 'Son of God' attributed to Jesus is a central theme in the New Testament that carries significant theological weight. One crucial instance where this title appears is in Luke 1:35:

> "The angel answered and said to her, "The Holy Spirit will come upon you, and the power of the Most High will overshadow you; for that reason also the holy Child will be called the Son of God"

This declaration serves as a mere label and reveals an essential aspect of Jesus' identity and mission. The angel's proclamation establishes Jesus' divine origin. He is more than a mere human; He is begotten by God. This divine conception marks a fundamental break from ordinary human lineage.

The significance of the title 'Son of God' becomes even more apparent when we consider its implications concerning Jesus' relationship with God the Father. In Matthew 3:17, during Jesus' baptism, a voice from heaven declares, "This is My beloved Son, with whom I am well pleased." This moment publicly affirms Jesus' divine sonship and His intimate relationship with the Father. It suggests a bond characterized by mutual love and shared purpose, highlighting the depth of their spiritual unity. The Father's public endorsement elevates Jesus beyond any prophet or king. It declares His special status within the divine world.

Tracing the 'Son of God' motif throughout the Gospels provides further insight into its profound implications. For example, in Mark 15:39, a Roman centurion, witnessing Jesus' crucifixion and subsequent death, exclaims, "Truly this man was the Son of God!" This acknowledgment from a Gentile soldier signifies a pivotal recognition of Jesus' divine identity. It emphasizes that Jesus' divinity is evident through miraculous acts and His sacrificial obedience unto death. This narrative thread across the Gospels reinforces that Jesus' sonship transcends ethnic and cultural boundaries.

Muslims are taught common misconceptions about the title 'Son of God.' Some suggest that 'Son of God' is purely metaphorical. It simply implies a close relationship with God without ascribing divine status. However, this view overlooks the consistent biblical portrayal of Jesus' unique nature and mission. For instance, passages like John 5:18 indicate that Jesus' claim to be the Son of God was understood by His contemporaries as a claim to equality with God (inciting accusations of blasphemy). Such reactions reveal that the term had a weightier implication than moral excellence or prophetic authority. It was a direct assertion of divinity.

To counter these misconceptions, we must consider the broader biblical context and the diverse applications of the title 'Son of God.' It is crucial to recognize that while other figures in the Bible, such as angels, kings, and the nation of Israel, are referred to as sons of God, Jesus' designation is distinct. The term applied to Jesus is more than honorific; it encapsulates His pre-existent divine nature, His incarnation, and His unique role in God's redemptive plan. Thus, equating Jesus' sonship with metaphorical language undermines the depth of His divine identity as consistently presented in the New Testament.

Providing a defense of the biblical understanding of Jesus as the Son of God involves addressing other objections raised by Muslims who question His deity based on this title. Muslims will cite verses like John 14:28, where Jesus states, "The Father is greater than I," to argue against His divine status. Understanding this passage within the broader theological framework shows that Jesus, in His incarnate form, acknowledged the Father's supremacy due to His voluntary submission and human limitations. Yet, this does not detract from His inherent divinity, as other passages affirm His equal standing with the Father. We will discuss this more later in the chapter.

Early Church's Belief in Jesus' Divinity

The early church's belief in the divinity of Jesus significantly shaped Christian theology. Central to this understanding was the development of key creeds. Most notable is the Nicene Creed in AD 325. The creed emerged during a period of intense theological debate over Jesus' nature. Convened by Emperor Constantine, the Council of Nicaea aimed to address the Arian controversy, which claimed that Jesus was a created being and not co-eternal with the Father. The council declared Jesus "begotten, not made" and "of one being with the Father." This creed established a foundational confession of Jesus' divine status. It emphasizes His co-eternity and consubstantiality with the Father, which rejects Arianism's claims.

Theological debates within early Christianity were not confined to Arianism. They also grappled with the nature of Jesus as both fully divine and fully human. These debates sought to articulate the mystery of the incarnation. How could Jesus be both God and man? Various heresies, such as Nestorianism, Apollinarianism, and Monophysitism, presented differing views. Nestorianism posited two separate persons in Christ, while Apollinarianism denied His human soul. Depending on the Muslim and their upbringing, they tend to argue from the heresies (note that they won't call them by name though).

However, the Council of Chalcedon in AD 451 addressed these controversies by affirming the doctrine of the hypostatic union—that Jesus is one person with two natures, fully divine and fully human. This definition aimed to preserve the integrity of both natures without confusion or division, providing a comprehensive Christological framework for the church.

Reflecting on these foundational doctrines shows their enduring influence on contemporary Christian theology and practice. The early church's fight to define and defend Christ's divinity laid the groundwork for later theological developments and councils. Today, the *Nicene Creed* remains a touchstone of the orthodox Christian belief. It is recited in many denominational liturgies and affirms the shared faith across various Christian traditions. This continuity underscores the importance of historical creeds in maintaining doctrinal unity and orthodoxy within Christianity. Additionally, the early church's rigorous theological reflections continue to inform modern discussions on the person and work of Jesus.

Theological debates around the nature of Jesus were multifaceted and often contentious. These debates were not mere academic exercises but were deeply connected to early Christians' lived faith and worship practices. The outcomes of these debates, enshrined in creedal formulations, provided clarity and cohesion for the Christian community. Understanding these debates helps us appreciate the complexities of early Christological discourses and the meticulous efforts to safeguard the apostolic faith. A faith that is being attacked today by the same rhetoric that the early church faced.

Alternative Interpretations to Jesus' Claims of Deity

As stated, Muslims often cite John 14:28, where Jesus states, "The Father is greater than I." Muslims argue this demonstrates a subordination that contradicts the assertion of Jesus' divinity. However, a counter-analysis reveals that this statement can be understood within the context of Jesus' earthly ministry. When Jesus speaks of the Father being greater, He refers to His incarnate state as a human being subject to limitations. He is not referring to His intrinsic inferiority in nature or essence.

For first-century Jews, monotheism was central, and any deviation from this concept would be perceived as blasphemous. Therefore, Jesus' declaration in John 14:28 needs to be seen through Jewish understanding. They recognized that His acknowledgment of the Father's greatness did not negate claims to equality in divinity but instead underscored His role within the divine plan of redemption.

When examining the whole counsel of Scripture, it becomes evident that Jesus' statements about His relationship with the Father must be harmonized with other declarations of His deity. For instance, Philippians 2:6-7 speaks of Jesus, who "as He *already* existed in the form of God, did not consider equality with God something to be grasped, but emptied Himself *by* taking the form of a bond-servant *and* being born in the likeness of men." This passage clarifies that Jesus' humility and submission were voluntary and part of the divine economy of salvation. Again, this reinforces His divine identity.

Muslims turn to passages like John 1:1, which states, "In the beginning was the Word, and the Word was with God, and the Word was God ," to challenge traditional readings. Some propose (mostly Jehovah's Witnesses and some Muslims) alternative translations, such as "the Word was a god," to diminish the assertion of Jesus' full deity. This interpretation, however, lacks substantial support both linguistically and contextually. The Greek text uses definite syntax affirming that the *Word* (*Logos*) shares the same essence as God - distinguishing yet uniting the Word with God.

An exegetical refutation of these alternative readings involves closely examining the original language and context. The term *Word* (*Logos*) holds deep philosophical and theological significance. It represents divine self-expression and creative power. John's prologue sets the tone for the entire Gospel. He presents Jesus as the pre-existent, divine *Logos* who became flesh (John 1:14). Reinterpreting this foundational verse undermines the coherence of the Gospel's portrayal of Jesus' divine nature.

In his letter to Colossae (Colossians 1:15-17), Paul describes Jesus as the "image of the invisible God" and asserts His role in creation and sustenance of all things. Such descriptions align with the high Christology present throughout the New Testament. A holistic approach to scriptural evidence reaffirms the consistent witness to Jesus' divinity. Muslims tend to isolate verses, but we must use all Scripture to embrace the broader narrative of God's revelation in Christ.

The consistency of the biblical witness concerning Jesus' divinity is evident when considering the totality of scriptural testimony. From Old Testament prophecies foreshadowing a divine Messiah (Isaiah 9:6) to New Testament affirmations such as Thomas' exclamation, "My Lord and my God!" (John 20:28), the biblical narrative upholds Jesus' divine status. The coherence of this testimony challenges attempts to fragment or isolate verses in ways that negate their collective affirmation of Jesus' deity.

Passages like Romans 9:5 explicitly refer to Christ, "who is over all," and Titus 2:13, which speaks of "our great God and Savior, Jesus Christ," provide further validation. Such references strengthen the case for Jesus' divinity and demonstrate that early Christian writers and communities consistently recognized Him as divine. This comprehensive review of biblical evidence underscores the unity and reliability of the scriptural witness to Jesus' divine identity.

When speaking with Muslims, it is also essential to engage in respectful dialogue and critical engagement, as they do not view Jesus' divine nature the same way Christians do. Muslims view Jesus as a prophet but not divine. You must show humility and intellectual openness. While presenting the biblical case for Jesus' divinity, fostering an environment of mutual respect allows for meaningful conversations and deeper understanding.

Summary

We explored the biblical evidence demonstrating that Jesus claimed His divinity and explained the theological implications of such claims. By analyzing key statements like " before Abraham was born, I am " *(John 8:58)* and " I and the Father are one, " *(John 10:30)* , we have seen how Jesus' declarations align with God's self-identification in the Old Testament. These proclamations were not merely metaphorical but carried profound significance. Jesus asserted his divine nature and eternal existence.

When Jesus said, "I am," He directly connected Himself to Yahweh's self-referential term in Exodus. This link between Jesus and the God of Israel revealed the continuity of God's revelation. Jesus situated His ministry firmly within God's redemptive plan. The reaction of the Jewish leaders, who considered these statements blasphemous, underscores the radical nature of His claims.

Jesus is THE Son of God. Key moments, such as the angelic announcement to Mary and the heavenly declaration during Jesus' baptism, highlighted His unique relationship with the Father. Despite some misconceptions that interpret this title metaphorically, the consistent biblical portrayal confirms Jesus as both fully God and fully man. This understanding is crucial for Christian theology and must be fully understood when speaking with Muslims.

The early church's belief in Jesus' divinity played a significant role in shaping Christian theology. Critical events like the Council of Nicaea established foundational doctrines. These councils and other events mentioned in Chapter Two defended the assertion of Jesus as co-eternal and the same with the Father. The creeds formed during these times continue to influence Christian thought and practice.

Understanding alternative interpretations of key passages related to Jesus' claims of deity is also essential. Muslims often cite verses like John 14:28 to challenge traditional beliefs. However, understanding these passages within their broader context reveals that Jesus' statements do not negate His divine status but indicate His voluntary submission during His earthly ministry. The holistic view of Scripture reaffirms the consistency of the biblical witness to Jesus' divinity.

Most Muslims have not read the Bible and have learned/ been taught many false misconceptions about Jesus' divinity. Understanding the biblical basis for Jesus' claims provides a foundation for respectful and informed discussions.

On a broader scale, acknowledging Jesus' divinity has significant theological and practical implications. It shapes the core of Christian worship, doctrine, and personal faith. It also influences how Christians view the nature of salvation. Only a fully divine Savior can bridge the gap between humanity and God.

Reflection

How do you interpret Jesus' declaration, "Before Abraham was born, I am" in John 8:58? How does the Greek term "egō eimi" deepen your understanding of Jesus' identity?

In what ways does Jesus' claim of unity with the Father in John 10:30 impact your understanding of the Trinity?

How do the "I AM" statements in the Gospel of John (e.g., "I am the bread of life," "I am the way, the truth, and the life") contribute to the overall portrayal of Jesus' divine identity?

How does the title 'Son of God,' as used in the New Testament, differ from its use in other contexts, such as referring to angels or kings? What unique significance does it have for Jesus?

How do early church creeds like the *Nicene Creed* help clarify and defend the doctrine of Jesus' divinity?

How do you reconcile passages like John 14:28 ("the Father is greater than I") with the overall biblical testimony to Jesus' divinity?

How can understanding first-century Judaism's cultural and theological context enhance our comprehension of Jesus' claims to deity?

What are some respectful and effective ways to engage in dialogue with Muslims about Jesus' divinity?

Chapter 4

God Cannot Have a Son

Understanding the Christian doctrine of the Sonship of Jesus is essential for engaging in meaningful discussions between Christians and Muslims. The term *Son of God* often causes confusion and misconceptions. In Islam, God's oneness (*Tawhid*) is a central tenet. By exploring the biblical context and addressing common misunderstandings, this chapter aims to explain how the title *Son of God* signifies more than just a familial relationship but instead speaks to Jesus' unique divine status and mission.

Son of God and Misconceptions

The term *Son of God* is significant in Christian theology, and understanding its meaning within a biblical context is crucial for addressing misconceptions. In the Bible, the phrase *Son of God* is not meant to imply a biological relationship as human fatherhood does. Instead, it signifies a unique positional and relational status that Jesus holds with God the Father. This title emphasizes Jesus' divine nature and his role in God's redemptive plan for humanity.

In the Old Testament, the concept of being a *son* of God was used metaphorically to describe individuals or groups that had a special relationship with God. For instance, Israel is referred to as God's firstborn son in Exodus 4:22. This clearly is a special bond rather than a literal offspring. The term also applied to kings and prophets who were seen as representatives of God's authority on earth. Understanding this metaphor helps clarify that the title "Son of God" for Jesus does not mean he is a physical offspring of God but asserts his divinity and mission as the Messiah.

We must explore how Jesus himself understood and used the term. While Jesus accepted and affirmed this title, he often referred to himself as the *Son of God* . This title emphasizes his messianic role and identification with humanity. For example, in John 10:34-36, Jesus defends his use of the term by referring to Psalm 82:6, which mentions humans as 'gods' due to their divine commissions. By highlighting this, Jesus clarifies that his claim to be the *Son of God* aligns with Jewish tradition and scripture without implying equality with God in a polytheistic sense.

Understanding the New Testament context further enriches our grasp of the term *Son of God* . The Gospels present Jesus' sonship as one rooted in divine approval and mission. This is particularly shown at his baptism and transfiguration, where God's voice affirms, " This is My beloved Son." (Matthew 3:17; 17:5) These instances underscore Jesus' unique relationship with the Father. It is a declaration rather than human lineage. This understanding protects the Christian belief in Jesus' divinity while maintaining monotheism.

Another aspect to consider is how early Christians interpreted and propagated this concept. The early church fathers and apostles consistently affirmed Jesus as the *Son of God* to articulate his divine nature and role in salvation history. Paul's letters emphasize that Jesus' sonship entails both his pre-existent divinity and his incarnation as a human being for the purpose of redemption - Galatians 4:4-5 and Romans 1:3-4. These verses stress the depth of the relationship between Jesus and God. They show Him as fully divine and fully human.

When engaging with Islamic objections, it's crucial to note the difference in understanding divine sonship. Islam strictly adheres to *Tawhid* (the absolute oneness of God) and rejects any notion of God having a son. Many Muslims interpret the term *Son of God* literally. They assume it implies a biological relationship that contradicts monotheism. However, clarifying the metaphorical and relational meanings within the biblical context can help bridge understanding. Christians view Jesus' sonship as a reflection of his divine mission and unity with the Father rather than a biological fact.

It is also essential to explore how Jesus' sonship fits into the broader narrative of the Bible. From Genesis to Revelation, the scriptures consistently portray God establishing covenants and relationships with humanity through chosen individuals. Jesus, as the ultimate fulfillment of these promises, embodies the perfect union between God and man. His title, Son of God, encapsulates this theological truth, making him the mediator of the new covenant and the revelation of God's love and grace.

The Trinity and the Sonship of Jesus

The concept of the Trinity (discussed in Chapter 5) is central to Christian theology and understanding the Sonship of Jesus. The Trinity refers to the belief that God exists as three persons in one essence: Father, Son, and Holy Spirit. This doctrine emphasizes that while each person of the Trinity is distinct—both co-equal and co-eternal—they share the exact divine nature.

Understanding the Trinity helps clarify the relationship between Jesus and God. In Christian belief, Jesus is the *Son of God* , but this does not imply a biological offspring. Instead, it signifies a unique, eternal relationship within the Godhead. According to John 1:1-14, Jesus (the Word) was with God from the beginning, and all things were made through Him. This passage indicates that Jesus' sonship is a spiritual and eternal truth. It is rooted in His divine nature and unity with the Father.

Moreover, the baptismal formula found in Matthew 28:19 - " baptizing them in the name of the Father and the Son and the Holy Spirit " - shows the critical role of the Trinity in Christian faith and practice. It signifies the believer's union with the Triune God.

The significance of the Trinity in explaining the Sonship of Jesus also lies in the relational dynamics within the Godhead. The Bible describes the Son as eternally begotten of the Father. Jesus is not created nor subordinate but equal in divinity. This distinction is vital to appreciating the depth of the relationship. As stated in John 3:16, " For God so loved the world, that He gave His only Son, so that everyone who believes in Him will not perish, but have eternal life. " As famously known in other translations, "only" can also be "begotten."

These descriptions of Jesus's Sonship clearly show an intricate and intimate connection—a connection where Jesus shares in the Father's essence and mission. The *Nicene Creed* affirms this by declaring Jesus as "Light from Light, true God from true God, begotten, not made, of one being with the Father." This theological framework shows that Jesus's Sonship is intrinsic to His divine identity and role within the Trinity.

The Father, Son, and Holy Spirit are one in essence but distinct in personhood and function. The doctrine of inseparable operations teaches that any act of God involves all three persons of the Trinity. For instance, in creation, the Father creates through the Son in the power of the Holy Spirit (Genesis 1, John 1:1-3). Likewise, in redemption, the Father sends the Son, who redeems through His life, death, and resurrection by the power of the Holy Spirit (Ephesians 1).

This unity and distinction ensure that Jesus' actions and teachings are understood as those of God Himself. Jesus was not merely a messenger or prophet. It reinforces the belief that through Jesus, believers encounter the fullness of God. The Trinitarian perspective is crucial for grasping the comprehensive role and identity of Jesus as the *Son of God* .

When speaking with Muslims about the Trinity, it is essential to use clear and relatable language. Terms like "begotten" must be unpacked to avoid misconceptions. Rather than implying creation or subordination, "begotten" within the Trinity signifies an eternal relationship. The Son emanates from the Father's essence. As theologian Christine Thornton explains, God's internal actions reflect His external works—meaning the relational dynamics within the Trinity manifest in how God reveals Himself and interacts with the world (Thornton, C., n.d.).

Misunderstandings from a Muslim Perspective

It is a common Islamic perception that Christians believe in multiple gods due to their use of terms like *Son of God* and Trinity. From an Islamic standpoint, the assertion that God has a son is seen as contradictory to the principle of *Tawhid* . Christians must understand this concept to communicate effectively about their beliefs without seeming disrespectful.

In Islamic theology, God is considered indivisible, unique, and singular. Making any notion of God having a son is polytheistic. This belief is deeply rooted in the Quranic verses that emphasize God's oneness and disclaim any partners or offspring. For instance, Surah Al-Ikhlas (*Quran 112:1-4*) unequivocally states that God does not beget nor is He begotten. When Muslims hear the term *Son of God* , they often interpret it through their theological lens. It is perceived as implying biological offspring - something explicitly denied in Islam.

It becomes imperative for Christians to clarify that the term *Son of God* does not imply a biological relationship but rather a unique, spiritual, and eternal relationship within the Trinity. When Christians call Jesus the *Son of God,* they are not suggesting that God physically fathered a child in a human sense. They are referring to a profound theological truth about the nature of Jesus Christ and His divinity. This distinction can help alleviate tension and misunderstanding from using familial language in describing divine relationships.

Another significant point of confusion is the belief that Christians think God had physical relations with Mary to produce Jesus. This misconception is both offensive and blasphemous to Muslims. Muslims revere Mary (Maryam) as one of the most pious women in history but vehemently reject any insinuation of a divine - human sexual relationship. In the Quran, Mary conceives Jesus miraculously by the command of God - without any physical interaction. This narrative aligns more closely with the Christian understanding of the virgin birth, where Mary conceives Jesus through the Holy Spirit's power.

To bridge this gap, Christians should emphasize the miraculous nature of Jesus' birth in both faiths while clarifying that references to Jesus as the *Son of God* denote His divine origin and mission rather than a literal parent-child relationship. Both traditions agree on the extraordinary manner in which Jesus was born. This is a point that can serve as common ground in discussions. Christians can address fears and correct misunderstandings without compromising their doctrinal integrity by focusing on shared beliefs and respectfully explaining differences.

In addition, Christians need to explain the concept of Jesus' sonship within the context of the Trinity. Many Muslims find the idea of the Trinity perplexing (as do many Christians) and incompatible with monotheism. They perceive it as a form of tritheism. However, the doctrine of the Trinity maintains that there is one God in three co-equal, co-eternal persons: the Father, the Son, and the Holy Spirit. This unified yet distinct existence does not imply multiple gods but a complex unity beyond complete human comprehension.

From personal experiences, I have found using analogies and examples resonates better with Muslims. For instance, the analogy of water existing simultaneously as liquid, ice, and steam helps to illustrate how one entity can have different forms without dividing its essence. Another example would be an egg - shell, albumen, and yolk. The egg is one but has three parts. Though these analogies are imperfect, they can aid in conveying the mystery of the Trinity without diminishing its profound theological implications. Clear communication and thoughtful comparisons are vital in addressing and dispelling the misconceptions surrounding the Trinity.

More Scriptural Jesus' Sonship

As already stated, John 3:16 states, " For God so loved the world, that He gave His only Son, so that everyone who believes in Him will not perish, but have eternal life. " This verse stresses the depth of God's love manifested through the giving of His Son. Jesus has a unique status as "only"

49

(begotten) and is distinguished from all other beings. Additionally, John 1:14 declares, " And the Word became flesh, and dwelt among us; and we saw His glory, glory as of the only *Son* from the Father, full of grace and truth. " Here, the term "only Son" draws attention to the exclusive nature of Jesus' Sonship. It shows His divine origin and intimate relationship with the Father.

Another essential passage is Matthew 3:17, during Jesus' baptism, where a voice from heaven proclaims, "This is My beloved Son, with whom I am well pleased." This public affirmation by God establishes Jesus' divine identity and His favor with the Father. Similarly, during the Transfiguration in Matthew 17:5, the voice from the cloud reiterates, "This is My beloved Son, with whom I am well pleased; listen to Him!" These instances confirm Jesus' unique position and authority derived from being the Son of God.

Exploring further, Jesus explicitly refers to God as His Father, creating a clear distinction in their relationship. In John 10:30, Jesus says, " I and my Father are one," suggesting an intricate unity yet maintaining personal distinctions within the Godhead. This statement supports the idea of an equal yet separate existence of Father and Son. Also, Jesus' prayer in John 17:21-22 asks believers to be one as He and the Father are one. Once again, Jesus illustrates the profound connection and unity shared between them.

Paul's writings also endorse this unique relationship. In Colossians 1:15-19, Paul describes Jesus as "the image of the invisible God, the firstborn of all creation," and says, "For it was the *Father's* good pleasure for all the fullness to dwell in Him." This passage affirms Jesus' preeminent role in creation and His embodiment of divine fullness. Hebrews reinforces His divine nature and ultimate authority as the Son. Hebrews 1:3 states Jesus as "And He is the radiance of His glory and the exact representation of His nature, and upholds all things by the word of His power."

These scriptures collectively assert Jesus' unique relationship with God as His Son. *Son of God* conveys an ontological connection and a functional role within the divine plan. The term affirms Jesus' divinity while maintaining the distinct personhoods within the Trinity. This theological framework provides a robust answer to objections regarding Jesus' Sonship.

Jesus' sonship in salvation history is another vital aspect to consider. His sonship is not merely a title but is deeply linked to God's redemptive plan. Romans 8:3 explains, "For what the Law could not do, weak as it was through the flesh, God *did* : sending His own Son in the likeness of sinful flesh and *as an offering* for sin, He condemned sin in the flesh . " Jesus, as God's Son, came in human form to fulfill the law's requirements and offer redemption. This act of incarnation underlines the necessity of understanding Jesus' divine and human natures working together to achieve salvation.

Galatians 4:4-5 states, "But when the fullness of the time came, God sent His Son, born of a woman, born under the Law, so that He might redeem those who were under the Law, that we might receive the adoption as sons *and daughters* ." This passage emphasizes Jesus' mission to redeem humanity and points out His dual role as fully divine and human. His sonship was crucial for the effectiveness of this mission. Jesus bridges the gap between God and mankind.

Understanding Jesus' unique relationship with God is fundamental for Christians engaging in dialogues with Muslims. Muslims reject the notion of divine sonship. Providing clear, scriptural evidence helps to articulate the Christian perspective accurately.

Summary

We have explored the Christian doctrine of Jesus' Sonship in light of Islamic objections. The biblical context of the term *Son of God* emphasizes that it does not imply a biological relationship but signifies Jesus' unique position and divine nature. This understanding is rooted in both the Old and New Testaments. In both Testaments, we see metaphorical usage that helps present Jesus' sonship as a declaration of his divinity and mission.

Jesus himself understood and used the term *Son of God* , and he frequently referred to himself as the *Son of Man* to underline his messianic role and shared humanity. By examining such instances, including references to Jewish tradition and scripture, we revealed that the title aligns with the biblical narrative without implying any physical relationship.

Understanding the Trinity is essential for grasping Jesus' sonship. Jesus' sonship exists within the context of the Trinity, a belief in one God in three distinct persons: Father, Son, and Holy Spirit. This complex unity does not suggest multiple gods but showcases an eternal relationship where the Son shares divinity with the Father and the Holy Spirit. This theological perspective provides clarity and reinforces Jesus' identity and role in the Christian faith.

When engaging with Islamic objections, it is essential to consider the differences in theological understanding. Islam's strict adherence to *Tawhid* , the oneness of God, leads many Muslims to interpret the term *Son of God* literally. It is vitally important to understand the significance of explaining that Christians see Jesus' sonship as a reflection of his divine mission and unity with the Father rather than a biological fact.

The scriptural evidence further establishes the unique relationship between Jesus and God. Verses from the Bible repeatedly affirm Jesus' special status. These passages show Jesus' divine origin and mission, and public affirmations support them during key moments like his baptism and transfiguration.

Understanding Jesus' Sonship requires a comprehensive look at biblical teachings, the Trinity, and historical interpretations by early Christians. Addressing Islamic objections involves clear communication about these theological concepts to foster mutual respect and comprehension. Recognizing the complexity and depth of Jesus' relationship with God allows for richer conversations.

Reflection

In what ways does the Old Testament's use of S *on of God* to describe individuals or groups provide insight into the title's significance for Jesus in the New Testament?

How do Jesus' references to himself as the *Son of Man* influence our understanding of his identity and mission?

How does the concept of the Trinity help clarify the relationship between Jesus and God the Father - especially in light of Islamic objections to divine sonship?

How can analogies like water in different forms (liquid, ice, steam) or an egg (shell, whites, yolk) aid in explaining the Trinity to those unfamiliar with the concept?

How do the public affirmations of Jesus' sonship during his baptism and transfiguration enhance our understanding of his unique relationship with God?

In what ways can the miraculous nature of Jesus' birth, as acknowledged in both Christianity and Islam, serve as a common ground for interfaith discussions?

How does the scriptural evidence from the Old and New Testaments reinforce the idea of Jesus' unique relationship with God and his role in the divine plan?

How can you effectively communicate the non-biological, metaphorical meaning of Jesus' sonship to Muslims while respecting their strict adherence to *Tawhid* ?

How does recognizing the complexity and depth of Jesus' relationship with God foster richer and more respectful conversations between Christians and Muslims about the nature of Jesus and his divine mission?

Chapter 5

Trinity Means Three Gods

Understanding the concept of the Trinity is essential for grasping the core of Christian theology. The doctrine states that God exists as three distinct persons - Father, Son, and Holy Spirit - yet remains one in essence. Based on upbringing and lessons taught, some Muslims believe the Trinity is - God, Jesus, and Mary. Trinity has sparked considerable debate. Muslims often claim that it implies the existence of multiple gods (polytheism). The goal of this chapter is to address such claims and provide a thorough explanation of how the Trinity represents unity within diversity rather than polytheism.

Understanding the Trinity Doctrine

Understanding the doctrine of the Trinity is crucial for comprehending the Christian faith. The concept of the Trinity states that God exists as three persons - Father, Son (Jesus Christ), and Holy Spirit - but is one in essence. This doctrine is foundational because it shapes the entire framework of Christian theology. It impacts Christians' understanding of God's nature, actions, and relationship with humanity. The Trinity reflects the unity and diversity of God's being and emphasizes that the divine persons are co-eternal, co-equal, and consubstantial.

The implications of the Trinity are vast and profound. For instance, the incarnation of Jesus Christ demonstrates the intimate involvement of the Triune God in human history. The Father sent the Son into the world to reveal divine love and bring salvation. This act shows the collaborative work of the Trinity. Each person plays a distinct yet harmonious role. Additionally, the Holy Spirit continues to guide and empower believers - reflecting God's ongoing presence in the Church's life.

In Christian practice, the Trinity influences worship, prayer, and the sacraments. Baptism, performed in the name of the Father, Son, and Holy Spirit, signifies initiation into the Trinitarian community. The communal and relational aspects of the Trinity serve as a model for Christian relationships and fellowship.

The Unity of God

The Triune nature of God emphasizes that the Father, Son, and Holy Spirit coexist in perfect unity. Matthew 28:19 commands believers to baptize in the name of all three persons, indicating their equal divinity and unified mission. Similarly, 2 Corinthians 13:14 highlights the grace of Jesus, God's love, and the Holy Spirit's fellowship. Paul showcases their distinct yet interconnected roles within the Godhead.

The Father is often viewed as the source or origin within the Trinity. He is the creator and sustainer of all things. The Father demonstrates His infinite power and wisdom. Jesus Christ, the Son, is God incarnate, who came to redeem humanity through His life, death, and resurrection. His role illuminates the deep compassion and sacrificial love within the Godhead. The Holy Spirit, the third person of the Trinity, is the presence of God active in the world today. The Holy Spirit sanctifies, guides, and empowers believers to live according to God's will.

These roles do not imply a hierarchy within the Trinity but depict different aspects of God's relationship with creation. Each person of the Trinity shares the same divine essence - making them inseparable and fully God. Recognizing this helps avoid the misconception of tritheism (which suggests three separate gods) and maintains the central tenet of Christian monotheism. There is only ONE God.

Biblical Passages Supporting the Trinity

The doctrine of the Trinity is supported by numerous biblical passages spanning the Old and New Testaments.

Genesis 1:26, where God says, "Let Us make mankind in Our image, according to Our likeness," hints at a plural aspect within the unity of God early in Scripture. Referring to the Tower of Babel in Genesis 11:7, God says, "Come, let Us go down and there confuse their language." The prophet Isaiah records in Isaiah 6:8, "Then I heard the voice of the Lord, saying, "Whom shall I send, and who will go for Us?" Then I said, "Here am I. Send me!" Although the complete revelation of the Trinity is more explicit in the New Testament, these Old Testament references set the stage for understanding God's complex nature.

In the New Testament, John 1:1 states, "In the beginning was the Word, and the Word was with God, and the Word was God." This passage clarifies that Jesus (the Word) is distinct from and at one with God the Father. John's Gospel emphasizes the interconnectedness and different roles of the Father, Son, and Holy Spirit. For example, John 14:26 describes how the Father sends the Holy Spirit in the name of Jesus. This indicates the cooperation and unity among the three persons.

Other passages, such as Colossians 2:9, assert that in Christ, "For in Him all the fullness of Deity dwells in bodily form," further confirming the divinity of each Trinitarian person. These scriptural references provide a comprehensive portrayal of the Trinity and highlight the continuity and coherence of this doctrine across both Testaments.

Common Objections and Analogies

Given the complexity of the Trinity, analogies can be helpful tools for better comprehension. As a caution, they must be handled carefully to avoid theological inaccuracies. One common analogy compares the Trinity to water, which can exist in liquid, solid (ice), and gas (steam) forms. This illustrates how one substance can manifest in three different states while remaining fundamentally the same.

However, it's essential to distinguish between modes and persons. Unlike water transitioning between states, each person of the Trinity coexists simultaneously and eternally. This distinction is crucial to avoid the heresy of modalism.

Modalism wrongly suggests that God merely switches modes or roles.

Saint Augustine offered an analogy using human faculties—memory, understanding, and will. Just as these aspects of the mind are distinct yet inseparable, so are the persons of the Trinity. Memory recalls knowledge, understanding interprets it, and will act upon it; none can function entirely apart from the others. This analogy aids in conceptualizing the distinct yet unified activity within the Godhead (Sica, C., 2019).

Another example mentioned in Chapter Four is the egg analogy. An egg consists of three parts - the shell, yolk, and albumen (white part). However, it is one egg. Another analogy is that of an apple: skin, flesh, and core. A three-leaf clover can be used to describe the Trinity. The sun is an effective analogy - the sun itself (God), light (Jesus), and heat (Holy Spirit). No matter the analogy, it is essential to remember that they all break down at some point because God is not a materialist being - He is immaterial.

Moreover, Christians point to the inherent plurality within Islamic belief itself—the eternal nature of the Qur'an. If the Qur'an, considered an eternal attribute of Allah, exists alongside Him, then some form of plurality within unity is implicitly acknowledged. This argument sheds light on the potential consistency between Islamic theology and the Christian concept of a triune God. It indicates that complexity does not necessarily negate unity (Answering Muslim Objections to the Trinity.

www.answering-islam.org.
, n.d.).

Engaging in respectful and informed conversations about the Trinity requires a balance of humility and openness. Approaching each discussion with a genuine desire to understand Muslims' perspectives establishes a foundation of mutual respect. It is important to listen actively and acknowledge the valid points raised by others. This creates an environment conducive to more meaningful and productive dialogue. From here, you can begin to break down barriers and false misunderstandings and eventually share the Gospel.

Misconceptions About the Trinity

One common misconception about the Trinity is that it implies the existence of three gods (polytheism). However, the doctrine of the Trinity unequivocally asserts that there is only one God in three persons. The unity of essence among the Father, Son, and Holy Spirit ensures that Christianity remains monotheistic. This concept is echoed in Deuteronomy 6:4, which declares the oneness of God: "Hear, Israel! The Lord is our God, the Lord is one!"

Rebutting accusations of polytheism involves explaining that God's threeness refers to persons, not separate beings. Each person of the Trinity shares the same divine substance. This means they are not three independent deities but one being in relational diversity. This unity in diversity is a profound mystery but aligns with the consistent biblical depiction of God's singular essence.

Muslims will use logic and math to try to destroy the Trinity. They argue that $1+1+1 = 3$ and not 1. However, the Trinity is more along the lines of $1x1x1 = 1$ or $1/1/1 = 1$. Who says it has to be an addition, not multiplication, division, or cube? Follow the Scripture and see what God says; He is our teacher and master.

Misunderstandings also arise when Muslims assume that praying to Jesus or invoking the Holy Spirit detracts from God's oneness. In Christian theology, addressing prayers to any person of the Trinity does not fragment God's unity but recognizes the distinct relational dynamics within the Godhead. Thus, Christian worship and prayer maintain the integrity of monotheism while honoring God's tri-personal nature.

Strengthening the Argument

Strengthening the argument for the theological coherence of the Trinity involves exploring how this doctrine enriches Christian understanding of salvation and divine relationships. Ephesians 1:3-14 illustrates that each person within the Triune God plays a distinct yet harmonious role in the work of salvation. The Father initiates salvation by choosing believers before the foundation of the world. The Son accomplishes redemption through His sacrificial death, and the Holy Spirit seals believers and guarantees their inheritance until the final redemption. This division of roles within the Trinity underscores the unique functions of the Father, Son, and Holy Spirit in the grand narrative of salvation.

The concept of divine relationship in the Trinity also provides profound insights into God's relational nature. Within the Trinity, there is perfect unity and mutual indwelling among the Father, Son, and Holy Spirit. This eternal relationship serves as a model for human relationships. It reflects divine love, cooperation, and unity. By contemplating the interrelationships within the Trinity, Christians can gain a deeper understanding of how love and community are intrinsic to God's nature. It emphasizes that God's essence is inherently relational. Humans are created in God's image to live in loving and harmonious relationships.

Tracing the development of Trinitarian theology through key councils and controversies reveals how early Christians grappled with and clarified the doctrine over centuries. As reviewed in Chapter 5, the Council of Nicaea in AD 325 was pivotal in defining the deity of Christ against Arianism. The *Nicene Creed* affirmed that the Son is "of the same substance" (homoousios) as the Father. This articulation was essential for maintaining the Trinitarian view that the Father, Son, and Holy Spirit are co-equal and co-eternal. The Nicaea Council solidified the theological foundation that the three persons share one divine essence.

In addition, the Council of Constantinople in AD 381 refined Trinitarian doctrine by addressing the nature of the Holy Spirit. This council expanded on the Nicene Creed and affirmed that the Holy Spirit is worshiped and glorified with the Father and the Son. This clarification was crucial in establishing the full divinity of the Holy Spirit. These councils demonstrate the Church's commitment to preserving the integrity of its core doctrines and show the gradual, reasoned process of theological development that culminated in a more precise articulation of the Trinity.

Illustrating how the Trinity influences Christian doctrine, worship, and community life helps Muslims understand its practical applications. In Christian worship, the Trinitarian formula is central - particularly in baptism as commanded in Matthew 28:19. Baptism in the name of the Father, Son, and Holy Spirit signifies entry into the Christian faith and reflects the fundamental belief in the Triune God. This practice roots the believer's identity in the relational dynamics of the Trinity.

In community life, the Church is seen as the body of Christ. This body mirrors the relational and cooperative nature of the Trinity. Each member of the Church has unique gifts and roles, and each contributes to the overall unity and mission of the community. This reflection of Trinitarian relationships fosters a sense of belonging, interdependence, and mutual support among believers. By embodying these principles, the Church demonstrates the lived reality of Trinitarian doctrine. The Church showcases how theological beliefs translate into tangible expressions of faith and community.

Summary

As we conclude the doctrine of the Trinity, we must be able to defend its claims of polytheism. We can show how the Father, Son, and Holy Spirit coexist in unity without compromising monotheism by examining biblical passages and analogies. It is also essential to discuss the implications of the Trinity for Christian worship, prayer, and community life.

Returning to the earlier point about the Trinity shaping Christian theology, it is important to reinforce that understanding God's Triune nature enhances our comprehension of divine relationships and salvation. Each person of the Trinity—Father, Son, and Holy Spirit—plays a distinct yet harmonious role in the redemptive story. They all showcase God's relational nature and His involvement in human history.

The Christian's current position is that the doctrine of the Trinity, while complex, remains a coherent and essential element of Christian belief. It provides a unified framework that explains the diversity within God's singular essence and maintains the integrity of monotheism. This perspective helps rebut accusations of polytheism and supports the theological consistency of the Trinity across both Testaments.

However, many Christians still find the concept challenging. It becomes challenging when engaging in dialogues with Muslims who emphasize strict monotheism. It is crucial to continue addressing these concerns respectfully and thoughtfully and using relatable analogies and clear scriptural references to convey the profound mystery of the Triune God.

As we conclude this chapter, let us contemplate the relational dynamics within the Trinity and their implications for our lives. The perfect unity and mutual love among the Father, Son, and Holy Spirit model how we should relate to one another. Embracing this divine example can inspire us to live in harmony and community.

Reflection

How does understanding the Trinity enhance your comprehension of the nature of God and His relationship with humanity?

What challenges do you face when explaining the concept of the Trinity to someone from a different faith background?

How do the Father, Son, and Holy Spirit's distinct roles impact your faith and understanding of salvation?

In what ways does the doctrine of the Trinity influence your approach to prayer and worship?

How do you respond to the common Muslim objection that the Trinity implies the existence of three gods?

How can analogies, despite their limitations, help explain the Trinity to someone who struggles with its complexity?

What are the implications of the Trinity for Christian community life and relationships within the Church?

How does the relational nature of the Trinity serve as a model for how we should relate to one another in our daily lives?

How can understanding the development of Trinitarian theology through key councils and controversies strengthen your faith?

How can you approach conversations about the Trinity with Muslims in a way that is respectful and open to mutual understanding?

Chapter 6

Jesus was Not Crucified and Atonement is Not Necessary

The crucifixion of Jesus and the necessity of atonement are pivotal topics within Christian theology. Both are often subjects of discussion and debate with Muslims. We will examine the historical evidence for the crucifixion and explore theological perspectives on why atonement is essential in Christianity. By comparing historical accounts from various sources with biblical narratives, we can provide a comprehensive understanding of the events surrounding Jesus' crucifixion and their significance in Christian doctrine when speaking with Muslims.

Historical Evidence for the Crucifixion
Establishing the historical evidence for the crucifixion of Jesus and its significance for Christian belief is crucial in understanding the foundations of Christian theology. One of the primary sources for verifying historical events is the writings of ancient historians. Roman historian Tacitus, who lived between AD 56-120, provides a critical historical testimony. In his work *Annals* , written around AD 116, Tacitus references the execution of Jesus under Pontius Pilate during the reign of Emperor Tiberius. This account supports the narrative found in the New Testament. Tacitus provides an external validation from a non-Christian source that acknowledges Jesus' crucifixion as a historical event. Tacitus' detailed description of the persecution of Christians by Nero further solidifies the credibility of his accounts related to early Christian history (Harrington, B., 2019).

Another significant historian, Josephus, a Jewish historian born in AD 37, also mentions the crucifixion of

Jesus. In his *Antiquities of the Jew* s, Josephus provides two references to Jesus. The first, known as the *Testimonium Flavianum* , briefly accounts for Jesus as a wise teacher who gained a following and was condemned to the cross by Pilate. Though there is debate regarding later Christian interpretations in this text, most scholars agree that a core, authentic reference to Jesus exists within Josephus' writings. These accounts by Tacitus and Josephus provide robust external evidence from contemporary sources that support the New Testament records of Jesus' crucifixion.

Reviewing biblical texts from the New Testament reveals a consistent narrative regarding the crucifixion of Jesus. All four Gospels—Matthew, Mark, Luke, and John—provide detailed accounts of the events leading up to and including Jesus' crucifixion. Each Gospel describes how Jesus was arrested, tried before Pontius Pilate, and ultimately crucified. These texts are central to Christian belief. They offer multiple independent attestations of the same historical event. For instance, Mark 15:24 states, "And they crucified Him," while John 19:18 similarly notes, "There they crucified Him, and with Him two other men, one on either side, and Jesus in between." These recurring accounts across various authors highlight the importance of the crucifixion in early Christian teachings.

Apostle Paul wrote the church in Corinth. In 1 Corinthians 15:3-4, Paul emphasizes that Christ died for sins, was buried, and rose on the third day. These events are foundational to the gospel message. Paul's epistles, some of the earliest New Testament writings, serve as additional corroboration from an entirely different set of documents. This internal consistency among diverse New Testament texts strengthens the argument for the historical reliability of Jesus' crucifixion.

The scholarly consensus on the historical reality of Jesus' crucifixion points towards its acceptance as one of the best-attested events in ancient history. Prominent scholars like Bart Ehrman, John Dominic Crossan, and E. P. Sanders agree that Jesus' crucifixion is a historical fact grounded in substantial evidence. Ehrman, for example, asserts that the crucifixion of Jesus is "one of the most certain facts of history" due to the multiple and independent attestations from both Christian and non-Christian sources. This widespread academic agreement stems from a rigorous examination of available evidence - historical documents and archaeological findings.

The criteria used by historians to evaluate the historical reliability of events, such as multiple attestation and enemy attestation, further support the authenticity of the crucifixion accounts. Multiple attestation refers to the presence of the same event recorded in different sources, such as the Gospels and works by Tacitus and Josephus. Enemy attestation highlights the fact that the crucifixion is acknowledged even by sources hostile to Christianity. Together, these criteria enhance the credibility of the crucifixion narrative. These discredit all claims that it is a theological construct without historical substance.

In addition to historical evidence, the crucifixion of Jesus holds profound significance for Christian belief. It represents the ultimate act of sacrifice. Jesus willingly endured immense suffering and death to atone for humanity's sins. Theologically, the crucifixion is viewed as the fulfillment of Old Testament prophecies, such as Isaiah 53, which speaks of a suffering servant who bears the sins of many. This connection between prophecy and fulfillment reinforces the belief in Jesus as the Messiah—more on this in the next section.

From a doctrinal perspective, the crucifixion is pivotal for concepts of redemption and salvation. Christians believe that through Jesus' death on the cross, the barrier between humanity and God caused by sin is removed, making reconciliation with God possible. Scriptures like Romans 5:8 state, "But God demonstrates His own love toward us, in that while we were still sinners, Christ died for us." This verse encapsulates the essence of Christian atonement theology. It illustrates how Jesus' sacrificial death embodies divine love and grace.

The Necessity of Atonement

According to biblical teachings, atonement in Christian theology is fundamental for addressing human sin. Atonement, by definition, refers to the reconciling of humanity with God through the sacrificial death of Jesus Christ. According to Scripture, human beings are inherently sinful and separated from God (Romans 3:23). Therefore, divine intervention is necessary for restoring this broken relationship. The New Testament emphasizes that Jesus' sacrificial death was the ultimate act of atonement. Jesus' death cleansed humanity from sin and opened the way for eternal life. For instance, John states, "He Himself is the propitiation for our sins; and not for ours only, but also for *the sins of* the whole world." (1 John 2:2)

Why does atonement matter? Because the theological perspective argues that without atonement, humanity cannot achieve true reconciliation with God. This perspective hinges on a critical tenet of Christian doctrine: God's holiness is incompatible with sin. Therefore, an adequate solution must address this incompatibility. Jesus' death fulfills this requirement by acting as a substitute. He bore the punishment for human sin. Hebrews states, "But now once at the consummation of the ages He has been revealed to put away sin by the sacrifice of Himself." (Hebrews 9:26) This Scripture shows the necessity of Jesus' atoning sacrifice as the means to bridge the gap between God and humankind.

Atonement also serves as a cornerstone in the formation of Christian identity. The belief in Jesus' sacrificial death and resurrection gives Christians assurance of forgiveness and hope for eternal life. It shapes ethical behavior. It encourages believers to live lives reflective of Christ's love and sacrifice. Atonement is not merely a doctrinal point but a transformational experience impacting how Christians perceive themselves and interact with the world around them.

Exploring theological perspectives emphasizing atonement's role in reconciliation with God reveals diverse interpretations. One prominent view is the substitutionary atonement theory. This theory states that Jesus acted as a substitute. He took on the penalties due for human sin and satisfying God's justice. Anselm of Canterbury notably articulated this view. Anselm asserts that only a being who is fully God and fully human could adequately restore the balance disrupted by sin. This perspective highlights the seriousness of sin and the lengths God would go to secure human redemption.

Another significant theological viewpoint is the moral influence theory. This theory sees Jesus' sacrificial death as the ultimate demonstration of God's love. Proponents argue that witnessing such profound love compels individuals to repent and seek a closer relationship with God. This theory stresses the relational aspect of atonement and how it motivates ethical living and spiritual growth.

The ransom theory suggests that Jesus' death was a ransom paid to liberate humanity from bondage to sin and Satan. Early church fathers like Origen and Gregory of Nyssa contributed to this understanding. They proposed that Jesus' death was part of a divine strategy to defeat evil forces. Each perspective offers unique insights into the multifaceted nature of atonement and enriches the theological dialogue about its significance.

Referencing Old Testament prophecies that foreshadow Jesus' sacrificial death adds depth to the atonement discussion. The Book of Isaiah presents a prophetic vision of a suffering servant who bears the sins of many. "But He was pierced for our offenses, He was crushed for our wrongdoings; The punishment for our well-being *was laid* upon Him, And by His wounds we are healed." (Isaiah 53:5) This passage vividly anticipates the sacrificial nature of Jesus' death. It portrays Him as the ultimate fulfillment of God's plan for redemption.

The Passover lamb in Exodus 12 serves as another powerful symbol of atonement. The blood of the lamb applied to Israelite doorposts saved them from judgment, mirroring how Jesus' blood saves believers from divine wrath. Paul draws this connection explicitly, referring to Jesus as "our Passover also has been sacrificed" (1 Corinthians 5:7). This typology reinforces the continuity between Old Testament sacrificial practices and New Testament beliefs about atonement.

Psalms and other prophetic books contain references Christians interpret as foreshadowing Jesus' redemptive work. Psalm 22, for example, depicts sufferings eerily similar to those Jesus endured during his crucifixion. These scriptural allusions create a cohesive narrative that aligns ancient prophecies with New Testament events.

Connecting these prophecies to Jesus' crucifixion showcases the fulfillment of divine promises and highlights the necessity of atonement. The Gospels often cite Old Testament prophecies to demonstrate that Jesus' suffering and death were part of God's redemptive plan. Matthew, for instance, frequently notes how specific actions or events in Jesus' life fulfill prophetic scriptures - establishing Jesus as the long-awaited Messiah. These connections strengthen the Christian claim that Jesus' atonement was divinely ordained and essential for salvation.

Understanding these fulfillments enhances the coherence of Christian doctrine. By linking Jesus' crucifixion with Old Testament prophecies, believers see a unified story of redemption that spans both Testaments. This continuity reassures Christians that their faith is grounded in historical and divine reality and not on arbitrary mythologies or wishful thinking.

Securing Salvation for Believers

According to Christian belief, humanity is inherently sinful and creates a rift between humans and God. This is original sin. Muslims do not believe in original sin but that everyone is born sinless. We sin as we grow and get older. Chapter Nine goes into greater detail on this objection.

Atonement serves as the bridge that repairs this broken relationship. Without atonement, the sin that separates humanity from God would remain unresolved. The separation leaves individuals estranged from divine grace.

The concept of atonement is deeply rooted in biblical teachings. It is seen as the act through which Jesus Christ, by his crucifixion, death, and resurrection, offered himself as a sacrifice to atone for the sins of humanity. This sacrificial act is believed to fulfill the requirements of divine justice while simultaneously demonstrating God's immense love for humanity. By willingly taking on the punishment for human sins, Jesus enables believers to be reconciled with God and opens the path to eternal life. The necessity of atonement is further strengthened by the belief that without it, there could be no forgiveness of sins or restoration of the broken relationship with God.

Understanding the profound connection between atonement and redemption requires an examination of critical biblical verses. Romans 5:8 succinctly highlights this connection: "But God demonstrates His own love toward us, in that while we were still sinners, Christ died for us." This verse encapsulates the essence of atonement and illustrates how Jesus' sacrificial death manifests God's love and provides a means for human redemption. Through his death and resurrection, Christ bears the penalty of sin, thereby redeeming humanity from the bondage of sin and death.

1 John 2:2 states, "and He Himself is the propitiation for our sins; and not for ours only, but also for *the sins of* the whole world." This passage emphasizes the universality of Jesus' atonement. The notion that Christ's sacrifice was sufficient to cover all sins highlights the boundless reach of God's grace. These biblical affirmations fortify the belief that atonement is indispensable for attaining salvation and point to its integral role in the Christian narrative of redemption.

Atonement addresses the fundamental issue of the separation between humanity and God due to sin. Sin creates a moral and spiritual divide, which prevents individuals from experiencing a full relationship with God. Atonement acts as a divine remedy that heals this breach. By addressing the root cause of separation—human sinfulness—atonement facilitates reconciliation and restores the harmonious relationship intended by God. Through repentance and acceptance of Jesus' sacrifice, believers return to right standing with God.

This reconciliation is not merely transactional but transformative. It signifies a renewal of the individual's relationship with God by fostering spiritual growth and alignment with divine will. The act of atonement is God's desire to restore communion with humanity. God is reflecting His enduring love and commitment to His creation. Therefore, the relational aspect of atonement goes beyond mere forgiveness; it involves restoring a deep, personal connection with the divine.

Objections to Atonement

Muslims do not believe in Jesus' sacrifice and, therefore, atonement. Chapter Nine goes into more detail on this and their salvation belief. However, one common objection to the need for atonement is the argument that a loving God should be able to forgive sins without any form of sacrifice. This perspective often stems from a misunderstanding of God's nature. Misunderstanding that His justice and holiness are considered secondary to His love. The question is why a benevolent deity would demand a sacrificial death as a prerequisite for forgiveness. Some argue this paints a picture of a vindictive God rather than one of infinite mercy and compassion. Such arguments suggest that divine forgiveness should mirror human forgiveness, which does not require payment or sacrifice from those being forgiven.

Responding to this objection requires understanding the integral relationship between God's attributes. Unlike human forgiveness, which may overlook justice for the sake of reconciliation, divine forgiveness involves upholding both justice and mercy. In Christianity, God's holiness necessitates that sin be addressed adequately because it violates the moral order He established. Atonement through Jesus' sacrifice resolves this by meeting the demands of justice—punishment for sin—while simultaneously expressing divine love through self-sacrifice. God's act of forgiving humanity through Jesus' death on the cross offers a comprehensive solution that reconciles His just nature with His loving character.

The theological rationale behind Jesus' sacrificial death centers on substitutionary atonement. According to this doctrine, Jesus took upon Himself the punishment due for humanity's sins, satisfying divine justice while providing a path to reconciliation with God. This can be illustrated by comparing it to a legal system where penalties must be paid for justice to be served. In this case, however, Jesus pays the penalty on behalf of all humanity. This act exemplifies not only justice but also the highest form of love. Jesus willingly endures suffering and death to restore humanity's relationship with God. This dual fulfillment of justice and mercy underscores the necessity of Jesus' sacrificial death within Christian theology.

Presenting reasoning for the necessity of atonement also involves the biblical portrayal of God's nature. In Christianity, God is depicted as both inherently just and boundlessly loving. His justice implies a steadfast intolerance for sin. Meanwhile, His love compels Him to provide a means for humanity's redemption despite its transgressions. The crucifixion of Jesus bridges this apparent paradox. Demonstrating how divine justice is satisfied through the penalty borne by Christ, divine love is manifested in offering salvation to sinners. This nuanced understanding helps believers reconcile the complex interplay of God's attributes.

In addition, theological principles like propitiation aid in grasping the necessity of atonement. Propitiation refers to appeasing God's righteous anger against sin. This theme is prevalent throughout the Bible. By offering Himself as a sacrifice, Jesus absorbs this divine wrath and restores peace between God and humanity. This concept differentiates Christian atonement from mere human attempts at reconciliation (work-based faiths). It emphasizes the gravity of sin and the profound lengths to which God goes to address it. Without such a sacrificial act, divine justice remains unfulfilled, and humanity remains estranged from God.

Scripture consistently points to the requirement of bloodshed for the remission of sins. Hebrews 9:22 states, "without the shedding of blood there is no forgiveness." The sacrificial rituals of the Old Testament foreshadowed the ultimate sacrifice of Jesus Christ. Throughout the New Testament, Jesus is portrayed as the Lamb of God who takes away the sins of the world (John 1:29). Jesus fulfilled the requirements laid out in earlier scriptures.

Finally, the apostolic teachings further clarify the essential role of atonement. Paul's epistles, particularly Romans and Corinthians, stress the significance and implications of Jesus' death. In Romans 3:25-26, Paul argues that God presented Christ as a sacrifice of atonement through the shedding of His blood - demonstrating His righteousness.

"Whom God displayed publicly as a propitiation in His blood through faith. *This was* to demonstrate His righteousness, because in God's *merciful* restraint He let the sins previously committed go unpunished; for the demonstration, *that is* , of His righteousness at the present time, so that He would be just and the justifier of the one who has faith in Jesus." - Romans 3:25-26

Similarly, 1 Corinthians 15:3 teaches that Christ died for sins in accordance with the scriptures. The crucifixion is a foundational tenet of the faith.

"For I handed down to you as of first importance what I also received, that Christ died for our sins according to the Scriptures" - 1 Corinthians 15:3

These texts provide a coherent scriptural narrative supporting the concept of atonement as central to Christian belief.

Summary

We have examined the historical and theological responses to the denial of Jesus' crucifixion and the necessity of atonement in Christian theology. By analyzing accounts from ancient historians like Tacitus and Josephus alongside New Testament texts, we have seen a robust body of evidence supporting the historical reality of Jesus' crucifixion. These accounts form the backbone of Christian belief and validate the crucifixion as a pivotal event not only historically but also theologically.

It becomes evident that Jesus' sacrificial death is integral to Christian doctrine. The concept of atonement addresses the inherent separation between humanity and God due to sin. Atonement provides a means for reconciliation through the sacrifice of Jesus Christ.

The current Christian position emphasizes that historical evidence and theological reflection affirm the significance of Jesus' crucifixion and atonement. This dual validation helps Christians understand the depth of their faith and offers a solid foundation when engaging with Muslims.

Muslims argue that divine forgiveness should not necessitate sacrifice and suggest a more straightforward expression of God's love. Understanding and thoughtfully responding to such objections can strengthen one's faith and ability to convincingly articulate the necessity of atonement.

Reflection

How does the historical evidence provided by Tacitus and Josephus enhance your understanding of the crucifixion of Jesus?

What significance do you find in the consistency of the crucifixion narrative across the four Gospels and the writings of Paul?

How do you reconcile the differing views on the necessity of atonement between Christianity and Islam?

How does the concept of atonement shape your understanding of justice and mercy in the context of your faith?

How do Old Testament prophecies, such as those found in Isaiah 53, influence your perception of Jesus' crucifixion and its fulfillment in the New Testament?

How would you respond to the objection that a loving God should be able to forgive sins without requiring a sacrifice?

What are the implications of viewing Jesus' sacrificial death through different theological lenses, such as substitutionary atonement, moral influence theory, or ransom theory?

How do you see the concept of atonement influencing Christian ethical behavior and spiritual growth?

How does the portrayal of Jesus as the Passover lamb and other typologies from the Old Testament enrich your understanding of atonement?

What challenges do you anticipate when discussing the necessity of atonement with Muslims, and how might you address these challenges?

Chapter 7

God Would Not Let a Prophet Like Jesus Suffer the Disgrace of the Cross

We will take the discussion in Chapter Six and the idea of atonement one step further. Addressing the perceived dishonor of the crucifixion requires understanding its significance within God's redemptive plan. The idea that God would not allow a prophet like Jesus to suffer the disgrace of the cross is pivotal in this discussion. Although seemingly shameful by worldly standards, the crucifixion plays an essential role in the divine narrative of redemption and salvation.

We will explore the theological underpinnings of suffering leading to redemption that draws parallels between Jesus' crucifixion and the trials faced by other biblical figures. We will revisit specific Old Testament prophecies that foretold the suffering Messiah that point to the fulfillment of Jesus' death.

Suffering and Redemption

Suffering leading to redemption is deeply embedded in biblical theology. This idea is pivotal in understanding the significance of Christ's sacrificial death on the cross. Throughout the Bible, we see that suffering often precedes spiritual growth and redemption. For instance, the trials faced by the Israelites during their exodus from Egypt ultimately led them to a deeper relationship with God. Similarly, Christ's suffering was not in vain but was integral to God's redemptive plan for humanity.

Christ's crucifixion is the ultimate expression of this redemptive suffering. Jesus' willing sacrifice on the cross serves a dual purpose: it fulfills Old Testament prophecies and exemplifies God's profound love for humankind. By bearing the weight of humanity's sins, Jesus opened the path to salvation for all who believe in Him. His suffering demonstrated that redemption often involves significant sacrifice and pain - a theme throughout the Scriptures.

Christ's sacrifice illustrates that something beautiful and redemptive can emerge through enduring pain and hardship. This is evident in how Jesus' crucifixion transformed the cross from a symbol of shame into one of hope and redemption. Believers are called to view suffering not as a punishment but as a potential pathway to deeper faith and ultimate redemption.

We can also draw parallels between Jesus' suffering and other biblical figures - such as Job and Jeremiah. Job's story is a profound example of unwavering faith amidst extreme suffering. Despite losing everything, Job's steadfastness led to his eventual restoration and deeper understanding of God's sovereignty. Similarly, the prophet Jeremiah endured significant hardship while carrying out his divine mission. His perseverance under oppression highlighted his commitment to God's will.

These stories resonate with Jesus' own suffering on the cross. Like Job and Jeremiah, Jesus endured immense pain and humiliation yet remained steadfast in His mission. These parallels reinforce that suffering can lead to profound spiritual growth and fulfillment of God's purposes when embraced with faith.

Understanding these connections helps believers and Muslims find meaning and strength in their own hardships. By studying these biblical examples, Christians can know that their suffering is not in vain but an opportunity to grow closer to God and fulfill their divine purpose.

The honor inherent in selfless love is another crucial aspect of Christian teaching. In a world that often equates honor with power and prestige, the sacrificial love displayed by Jesus stands in stark contrast. His willingness to lay down His life for others represents the highest form of honor and selflessness. Jesus teaches us that true honor comes from serving and loving others unconditionally.

Jesus' act of selfless love on the cross redefined what it means to be honorable in God's eyes. It showed that the greatest honor lies in humility and service rather than worldly achievements or accolades. Jesus set an example for believers to follow by choosing to suffer and die for humanity. Jesus emphasized that true greatness is achieved through loving sacrifice.

Followers of Christ are encouraged to embody the same selfless love daily. By prioritizing the needs of others and embracing humility, believers reflect Jesus' divine attributes and fulfill their calling to live as His disciples.

God's sovereignty and His purposes through suffering are essential themes in understanding the crucifixion. Jesus' journey to the cross was not a series of unfortunate events but a deliberate part of God's redemptive plan. From the outset, Jesus knew He was destined to suffer for the greater good of humanity. His suffering also demonstrated the extent of God's control over the unfolding of divine history.

Jesus' Suffering Aligns with God's Redemptive Plan

We have examined this in previous chapters, but it is worth revisiting for repetition and knowledge. Prophecies found in Psalm 22 and Isaiah 53 provide a profound understanding of how Jesus' suffering on the cross aligns with God's redemptive plan. Psalm 22 is particularly striking as it begins with the words "My God, my God, why have You forsaken me?" - words that Jesus himself echoes on the cross. This psalm not only foretells various aspects of the crucifixion, like the piercing of hands and feet but also predicts the mocking and scorn Jesus faced. By fulfilling these prophecies, Jesus' crucifixion is imbued with divine intention.

Isaiah 53, often referred to as the Suffering Servant passage, further illustrates this connection. The chapter vividly describes a figure who bears the pain and suffering of others while taking on their iniquities and being "pierced for our offenses." This prophecy aligns closely with the New Testament accounts of Jesus' suffering and crucifixion. By comparing these ancient texts with the events of Jesus' death, we can see a clear and purposeful fulfillment of God's promises through the sufferings of Jesus. Far from being a random act of brutality, the crucifixion is portrayed as a necessary part of the divine narrative leading to redemption.

These prophecies point to the notion that Jesus' suffering was not a sign of defeat or disgrace but a testimony to God's overarching plan of redemption. The fulfillment of such detailed and specific prophecies reassure believers that God's control over history is sovereign. It demonstrates that what happened on the cross was neither unexpected nor futile; instead, it was a meticulously orchestrated event designed to achieve ultimate victory over sin and death.

The Apostle Paul eloquently states this victory in his letters. 1 Corinthians 15:55-57 he celebrates the victory over death. The resurrection of Jesus, which follows His crucifixion, signals the defeat of death itself. Believers have hope of eternal life. This transformative power of the cross changes its perception from a mere instrument of death to a powerful symbol of life and hope. It signifies that through Jesus' sacrifice, believers are freed from the bonds of sin and granted the promise of new, everlasting life.

Sin created a chasm between humans and God. Human efforts alone cannot mend this separation. The crucifixion serves as the unique bridge across this divide. In Ephesians 2:13-16, Paul explains through Jesus' blood, we are brought near to God. Enmity is abolished - creating peace and unity between God and mankind.

This bridging act of the crucifixion also paves the way for forgiveness. Through Jesus' death, the penalty for sin is paid in full. Believers have received forgiveness and entered into a restored relationship with God. This concept of atonement shows that Jesus' suffering and subsequent crucifixion were purposed to repair the broken relationship between humanity and the Divine. The crucifixion thus becomes a crucial element in the narrative of redemption. God has proactively drawn humanity back to Himself.

Finally, the cross fosters a sense of belonging and adoption into God's family. According to Galatians 4:4-5, through Jesus' sacrificial death, believers are redeemed and adopted as sons and daughters of God. This familial bond illustrates the relational aspect of the crucifixion. It does not emphasize just the legal forgiveness of sins but also an intimate restoration of fellowship with God. It affirms that through the cross, individuals are not merely pardoned but are actively welcomed into the loving fold of God's family.

Reflecting on the depth of God's love demonstrated through Jesus' willingness to suffer for the salvation of all unveils the extraordinary nature of divine love. John 3:16 captures this sentiment succinctly: "For God so loved the world, that He gave His only Son, so that everyone who believes in Him will not perish, but have eternal life." Jesus' willingness to endure the agony of the cross is the ultimate expression of God's sacrificial love.

Wisdom Behind Jesus' Sacrificial Death

Understanding the differing perspectives between worldly views of suffering and shame and God's redemptive purposes is crucial. In human society, enduring suffering and public shame is often seen as a disgrace and signifying failure or punishment. However, these moments can hold significant purpose and value from a divine perspective. Christ's sacrificial death on the cross was not a moment of defeat but a profound act of love and redemption within God's ultimate plan for humanity.

The crucifixion of Jesus transformed what was seen as a symbol of shame - public execution via the cross - into a beacon of salvation and hope. Historically, crucifixion was reserved for the most heinous criminals. The crucifixion was intended to be a public spectacle that instilled fear and maintained order. Through His sacrifice, Jesus subverted this narrative. By willingly embracing the cross, He turned it into a symbol of triumph over sin and death and demonstrated His role as the Savior. This transformation invites us to see beyond immediate appearances and recognize the more profound spiritual realities at play.

Understanding the purpose behind the crucifixion requires faith and trust in God's sovereign plan. And yes - it defies human logic. God's ways are higher than ours, and His plans often surpass our understanding. The cross embodies this truth. It challenges believers to embrace a perspective that sees beyond human wisdom. Trusting in God's sovereignty means believing that His plan, despite its apparent paradoxes, leads to ultimate good. Embracing this trust is essential for deepening one's faith and grasping the profound mystery of the cross.

Encouraging deeper reflection on the profound truths revealed through the cross of Christ calls us to go beyond surface interpretations. The cross represents the intersection of justice and mercy. It is where God's righteous judgment against sin meets His boundless love and grace for humanity. Reflecting on this helps believers appreciate the depth of God's love and the lengths He went to reclaim His creation. It challenges us to live in response to this love, embodying the sacrificial nature of Christ in our daily lives.

Reinterpreting symbols of shame into symbols of salvation and hope is a central tenet of the Christian faith. Jesus took the cross, a tool of Roman humiliation and death, and turned it into a sign of ultimate victory. For Christians, the cross now stands as a reminder of God's power to transform even the darkest circumstances into sources of light and hope. This shift encourages believers to look at their own trials through the lens of faith and see the potential for God's redemptive work in every hardship.

Emphasizing the need for faith and trust in God's plan involves recognizing that human understanding is limited and often flawed. True faith requires believing in God's goodness and wisdom even when we cannot fully comprehend His methods. The crucifixion, viewed through the lens of faith, reveals God's commitment to humanity's salvation and His ability to bring about good from inherently evil or nonsensical situations. This call to trust is not blind. It is founded on recognizing God's past faithfulness and promises for the future.

Equipping for Theological Challenges

To offer a framework, we first need to examine critical biblical passages highlighting the cross's centrality in Christian theology. Paul's letters extensively cover the importance of the cross. For instance, in 1 Corinthians 1:18, Paul states, "For the word of the cross is foolishness to those who are perishing, but to us who are being saved it is the power of God." This passage shows how the cross serves as the ultimate revelation of God's power and wisdom and how it transcends human understanding and expectations.

The Gospels provide detailed narratives on the passion of Christ. They all emphasize that his suffering and crucifixion were foretold and necessary for salvation. Mark 10:45 explicitly states, "For even the Son of Man did not come to be served, but to serve, and to give His life as a ransom for many." Jesus foreshadows the sacrificial nature of His death and makes it clear that his crucifixion was an integral part of God's redemptive plan.

Romans 5:6-10 illustrates why Jesus' death is fundamental to Christianity. It elaborates on how Christ's sacrifice reconciles humanity with God. Therefore, understanding these texts helps believers understand why the crucifixion is not a sign of defeat but the cornerstone of their faith.

Communicating the theological depth of the cross effectively in discussions with Muslims requires finesse. One important tip is to start by acknowledging the seeming paradox of a crucified God. Recognizing this initial point of contention allows for a more honest and open dialogue. It's also helpful to draw analogies from literature and history. Self-sacrificial deeds often resonate deeply with people, providing a bridge to explain the concept of atonement.

Also, stressing the historical reliability of the crucifixion can bolster its credibility. Revisit Chapters One and Six for more details and explanations. Highlighting how non-Christian sources like Tacitus and Josephus corroborate the Gospel accounts underscores the event's historicity. This external validation makes the theological claims more approachable for Muslims. Offering personal testimonies (the most powerful one is yours!) of transformation due to embracing the cross's message is powerful. Christians are called to live out the principles of humility and service exemplified by Jesus. This means prioritizing others' needs, forgiving wrongs, and showing grace in everyday interactions.

Share stories of people who have forgiven grievous wrongs or sacrificed personal comfort for the well-being of others, highlighting the transformative power of embodying the cross. These stories serve as modern-day testimonies to the enduring relevance of Jesus' example.

Community engagement, where Christians participate in acts of kindness and social justice, reflects the cross's influence. Projects aimed at alleviating poverty, supporting marginalized groups, or fostering reconciliation are concrete ways to manifest the transformative love signified by the crucifixion.

Challenge yourself and reflect on how the message of the cross shapes your beliefs, attitudes, and actions. How does the reality of Jesus' sacrifice change your understanding of justice and forgiveness? In what ways can you demonstrate sacrificial love in your daily environment?

Inspire to have a more profound commitment to following Christ's example of sacrificial love and humility. Practice fasting, consecrated prayer, and acts of service to draw attention back to the essence of the Gospel message.

Summary

The crucifixion has an undeniable place in God's redemptive plan. The Bible shows suffering as a precursor to redemption and that Christ's sacrificial death is the ultimate example of this principle. Examples like the Israelites' exodus, Job's trials, and Jeremiah's perseverance, we see that suffering has always been part of the divine narrative leading to spiritual growth and fulfillment.

Clearly, Jesus' sacrifice fulfills ancient prophecies and exemplifies God's profound love for humanity. His suffering transforms the cross from a symbol of shame into one of victory. Redemption often involves significant pain and sacrifice.

The crucifixion aligns with Old Testament prophecies - Psalm 22 and Isaiah 53. This alignment reassures believers of God's sovereignty and intentionality and highlights that Jesus' suffering was neither random nor futile.

The tension between the worldly view of suffering and shame versus God's purposes invites a deeper trust in divine wisdom. God's ways often surpass human logic. By embracing this trust, believers can find strength and meaning in their own hardships. We see them as opportunities for spiritual growth rather than mere punishments.

Jesus' sacrifice challenges societal values that equate honor with power and prestige. It encourages Christians to embody sacrificial love and service in their daily lives.

Consider how Jesus' act of selfless love on the cross redefined what it means to be honorable in the eyes of God. Reflect on how this profound truth can reshape your beliefs, attitudes, and actions. How can the message of the cross influence your approach to justice, forgiveness, and humility?

Reflection

How does understanding the crucifixion as part of God's redemptive plan change your perspective on suffering and hardship in your own life?

In what ways do the stories of Job and Jeremiah help you see the significance of Jesus' suffering and sacrifice?

How does the concept of honor and disgrace in Jesus' crucifixion challenge your views on what it means to be honorable in God's eyes?

How do Old Testament prophecies like Psalm 22 and Isaiah 53 influence your understanding of Jesus' crucifixion and its necessity?

What personal experiences or examples from history resonate with the idea of self-sacrificial love exemplified by Jesus on the cross?

How do you respond to the idea that God's ways often surpass human understanding, particularly in the context of the crucifixion?

How can you demonstrate sacrificial love and humility in your daily life?

How does the crucifixion transform your view of suffering from a punishment to a potential pathway for spiritual growth and redemption?'

How can the message of the cross influence your approach to justice, forgiveness, and reconciliation in your relationships and community?

What practical steps can you take to embody the principles of sacrificial love and service in your interactions with others?

Mitchell Beecher

Chapter 8

Saved by Deeds and Not by Grace

Contrasting concepts of salvation based on grace versus works invite a closer examination of theological differences between Christianity and Islam. Understanding these differences is crucial when discussing salvation with Muslims. Christian doctrine emphasizes salvation through grace, portraying it as an unearned gift from God. Islam teaches the significance of deeds in achieving righteousness and divine favor. We will explore these core tenets and provide a clear understanding of how each religion perceives the path to salvation.

Biblical Teachings on Grace and Faith

Grace is a central aspect of Christianity. It emphasizes God's unmerited favor towards humanity. Unlike other religious concepts, where divine favor may be seen as something to earn, grace in Christianity highlights the idea that God's love and blessings are given freely. It is given without condition based on human actions. This concept can be traced back to various biblical scriptures, where God extends His mercy and kindness solely out of His compassion and love.

One pivotal aspect of Christian grace is its accessibility to all people. ALL PEOPLE regardless of their past sins. Anyone can come to God, seek forgiveness, and receive His grace. It directly challenges the notion that one must first achieve a certain level of righteousness through deeds before becoming worthy of divine favor. Instead, grace asserts that God's love is unconditional and extends to those who feel most unworthy.

Grace provides believers with assurance and hope. In Islam, a works-based religion, there is extreme uncertainty of salvation and entering paradise. Knowing that salvation depends not on their ability to perform good deeds but on God's unwavering grace gives Christians a profound sense of security. This assurance fosters a stronger, more resilient faith amid life's trials and tribulations because they trust in a loving God who does not keep score but instead offers everlasting mercy.

Faith is crucial in receiving God's grace and experiencing salvation. Faith acts as the conduit through which individuals accept and embrace the divine gift of grace. Faith, therefore, becomes the response to God's initiative. Believers can tap into the transformative power of His mercy. Without faith, the concept of grace remains theoretical and distant rather than practical and personal.

Faith is also essential in building and nurturing a relationship with God. Through faith, believers demonstrate their trust in God's promises and dependence on His providence for salvation. This trust sustains them through difficult times and reassures believers of God's presence and purpose for their lives. Faith serves as an initial step towards embracing grace and a continual practice deepening one's spiritual journey.

Faith aligns believers with Christ's redemptive work. Through faith, Christians acknowledge Jesus's sacrificial death and resurrection. This acknowledgment forms the bedrock of Christian doctrine and sets it apart from Islam. By placing faith at the center, Christianity emphasizes a life led by trust in divine grace rather than reliance on human merit.

Above all, grace is a gift freely given by God and cannot be earned through human efforts. This principle starkly contrasts Islam, which advocates for earning merit or favor through actions and deeds. According to Christian teachings, no good behavior or charitable deeds can secure a person's place in heaven; only through accepting God's grace can one attain salvation.

Rather than performing good works to earn salvation, Christians are encouraged to live righteously out of gratitude for the grace they have received. This shift from a transactional to a relational approach to spirituality emphasizes genuine transformation over compliance with religious laws or rituals.

Additionally, this perspective on grace cultivates humility among believers. Recognizing that salvation is not something they can achieve on their own diminishes pride and self-righteousness. Instead, it instills a sense of awe and appreciation for God's boundless compassion. Christians must rely entirely on His mercy and love rather than their abilities or accomplishments.

Finally, faith empowers believers to live out their salvation through obedience and spiritual growth. When Christians trust in God's promises, they are more likely to follow His commandments and seek to align their lives with His will. This obedience is not borne out of fear of punishment but rather from a heartfelt desire to honor the God who has graciously saved them. As their faith grows, they become more attuned to God's direction, wisdom, and power.

Paul vs. James on Faith and Works

Muslims tend to bring up both Paul and James and position arguments that it is by works we are saved. In addition, they state that Paul corrupted the true message of Jesus, and Christians follow Paul's teachings and not Jesus.

Paul stresses that salvation is by faith alone and not from works of the Law. In Romans 3:28, Paul clearly states, "For we maintain that a person is justified by faith apart from works of the Law." This assertion underlines that human efforts or adherence to the Law cannot earn salvation. Instead, it is through believing in Jesus Christ and his sacrificial death that one is justified before God. Paul's perspective challenges the notion that following religious rituals or moral codes can secure divine favor.

Paul teaches the sufficiency of Christ's sacrifice for the believer's justification. In Galatians 2:16, he proclaims that "a person is not justified by works of the Law but through faith in Christ Jesus." Here, Paul reiterates that Christ's atoning death and resurrection are adequate for salvation. Believers are invited to trust wholly in this divine provision rather than relying on their righteousness. This reliance on Christ fosters a sense of humility and gratitude. Salvation is a gift from God and not a reward for human achievements.

According to Paul, faith leads to a transformed life marked by obedience and good works. He urges believers to live out their faith actively and visibly and embody the values Jesus taught. For instance, Ephesians 2:10 states, "For we are His workmanship, created in Christ Jesus for good works, which God prepared beforehand so that we would walk in them." This highlights that while faith initiates salvation, it inevitably inspires a life committed to good deeds. Good works are seen not as the means to salvation but as natural outpouring.

On the other hand, James stresses the connection between faith and works in authentic Christian living. According to James 2:17, "Faith also, if it has no works, is dead, *being* by itself." James argues that genuine faith manifests itself through actions. These actions reflect the transformative power of belief in Christ. He challenges Christians to demonstrate their faith tangibly. This perspective underscores the importance of a holistic approach to faith by integrating conviction with practice.

James contends that genuine faith naturally produces good works as evidence of salvation. In James 2:26, he writes, "For just as the body without *the* spirit is dead, so also faith without works is dead." This analogy illustrates that faith and works are inseparable; just as a body without a spirit is lifeless, so is faith without corresponding actions. Works, therefore, are the fruits of a sincere and lively faith. These works confirm the believer's commitment to God's will. James' teaching emphasizes that actions speak louder than words when demonstrating faith.

For James, works are not a means of earning salvation but a manifestation of true faith. He asserts that an active, compassionate, and obedient life is the hallmark of a faithful Christian. Practically, this means caring for those in need, acting justly, and living ethically. By advocating for a faith that works through love, James invites believers to live out their convictions robustly and dynamically.

Ultimately, both Paul and James offer valuable insights into the nature of Christian salvation. Paul champions faith as the key to justification. James calls attention to the necessity of works as evidence of genuine faith. Rather than being contradictory, their teachings provide a comprehensive framework for understanding the interplay between belief and behavior in the Christian life.

Considering these perspectives, Christians can appreciate the fullness of their faith journey. They are called to embrace the grace offered through Christ's sacrifice and manifest this faith in their daily lives through acts of love and service. This balanced approach ensures a robust and dynamic expression of their beliefs. Christians can have full confidence that Paul and James are not contradicting each other—no matter the Islamic argument.

Grace in the Life of Jesus

Jesus should grace through his interactions with social outcasts and sinners. He extended forgiveness and compassion without prejudice. His actions defied societal norms and demonstrated that grace is available to all.

One poignant example is found in Luke 7:47, where Jesus forgives a woman known to be sinful.

"For this reason I say to you, her sins, which are many, have been forgiven, for she loved much; but the one who is forgiven little, loves little." - Luke 7:47

The woman washes His feet with her tears and wipes them with her hair - an act of deep humility and repentance. Jesus acknowledges her faith and forgives her sins. By doing this, He illustrates that grace is not earned but given freely. This encounter highlights Jesus' revolutionary approach to grace. He does not condemn but offers a path to redemption through sincere repentance. It shows that no one is beyond the reach of God's grace.

The Parable of the Prodigal Son (Luke 15:11-32) profoundly illustrates the depth of God's grace towards repentant hearts. In this parable, a wayward son squanders his inheritance on reckless living but ultimately returns home in desperation. Instead of reprimanding him, the father welcomes him back with open arms and celebrates his return. This narrative captures the concept of grace as unconditional love and forgiveness. Regardless of one's past mistakes, the father's joy in restoring his lost son reflects God's delight in welcoming repentant sinners into His embrace.

Jesus' parables are rich with these themes. He continually reinforced the message that grace is foundational to the Christian faith. Through stories like the Prodigal Son, Jesus communicates that God's grace surpasses human understanding and limitations. It challenges believers to view others with the same compassionate lens. These parables teach that grace is not about fairness or merit but God's boundless love and mercy for humanity. By embracing this perspective, Christians are called to extend grace to others and reflect the divine love that they have received.

In John 8:7, when a woman caught in adultery is brought before Him, Jesus famously says, "He who is without sin among you, let him *be the* first to throw a stone at her." When no one condemns her, Jesus tells the woman in verse 11, "I do not condemn you, either. Go. From now on do not sin any longer." This incident highlights Jesus' mission to offer salvation to all. His refusal to condemn but instead provide a chance for transformation reveals a profound compassion that breaks down barriers of judgment and exclusion.

Jesus' unconditional love and compassion were evident in his daily ministry. He healed the sick (Matthew 4:23), fed the hungry (Mark 6:33–44), and comforted the distressed (John 14:1-6). These acts of kindness and mercy were not just miracles but manifestations of divine grace that aimed to restore dignity and hope to the afflicted. By addressing physical and spiritual needs, Jesus demonstrated that God's love is holistic. His ministry continually invited people to experience God's grace daily.

In Matthew 9:13, Jesus states, "I desire compassion, rather than sacrifice,' for I did not come to call the righteous, but sinners." This declaration challenges conventional notions of righteousness and underscores God's inclusive redemption plan. Jesus' emphasis on mercy over ritual sacrifice reveals a shift from legalistic adherence to laws towards a relational understanding of faith rooted in compassion and grace. It calls believers to prioritize acts of love and mercy over rigid observance of religious practices.

Misunderstandings About Christian Salvation

Muslims often say that Christians can go on sinning their whole lives because they simply stick it on Jesus, ask for forgiveness, and then continue to live in sin (iniquity). They claim believers have a free license to sin. However, grace does not undermine accountability. Believers are still accountable for their conduct (Romans 6:1-2). While salvation is by grace through faith, believers must recognize the continued importance of their actions. Paul addresses a common misconception that grace permits a free-for-all lifestyle. He states that believers should not continue in sin just because grace abounds. This passage highlights the need for moral responsibility even under grace.

Accountability under grace stresses the transformative nature of salvation rather than external observances. Believers who genuinely experience God's grace naturally seek to align their lives with His teachings. Grace does not nullify the need for ethical living but intensifies it by providing the foundation and motivation for righteous behavior. This accountability is not rooted in fear of punishment but in gratitude for the transformative power of grace.

Christians living under God's grace involves continual self-examination and growth. Grace provides the spiritual resources needed to make progress in personal holiness. This ongoing process demonstrates the intricate balance between grace and accountability. By being mindful of their conduct, believers can effectively represent how the grace of God has impacted their lives.

Works flow naturally from a heart transformed by grace and are evidence of genuine faith. Again, Ephesians 2:10 clarifies that we are created in Christ Jesus for good works, which God prepared beforehand. This idea reveals that while good works do not earn salvation, they are a natural outcome of a heart changed by grace. A life marked by good deeds validates the sincerity of one's faith.

Grace empowers believers to live righteously and fulfill God's intended purpose for their lives. Titus 2:11-12 points out that divine grace brings salvation and instructs believers to renounce ungodliness and worldly passions.

"For the grace of God has appeared, bringing salvation to all people, instructing us to deny ungodliness and worldly desires and to live sensibly, righteously, and in a godly manner in the present age..." - Titus 2:11-12

This empowerment expresses that grace is not passive but actively involved in the believer's sanctification process. It equips them to lead lives that reflect God's holiness and purpose.

This shifts the focus from human effort to divine enablement. Believers do not strive for righteousness in their strength; instead, they rely on God's grace to mold their character and guide their actions. Grace becomes the catalyst for spiritual growth. Believers are able to reach their full potential in fulfilling God's plan. This understanding dispels misconceptions that grace is a license for complacency or laziness.

The power of grace fosters resilience and perseverance among believers. In difficult moments, grace sustains and provides the strength to remain steadfast. By relying on grace, Christians can overcome challenges and temptations. This continued reliance on divine grace is vital in enabling righteous living and achieving God's purposes.

The relationship between faith, grace, and works forms a harmonious framework for Christian living. James 2:24 illustrates that a person is justified by works and not by faith alone.

"You see that a person is justified by works and not by faith alone." - James 2:24

This statement clarifies the interplay between faith, grace, and works. Faith initiates the relationship with God, grace sustains it, and works to demonstrate its authenticity.

In this framework, faith without works is incomplete, and grace without accountability loses its transformative power. James's comprehensive approach ensures that Christian living remains balanced. This harmony prevents any extremes and ensures that neither faith nor works are overemphasized at the expense of the other. Instead, they coexist, each reinforcing and validating the other.

Summary

Christians are saved by grace through faith. It is out of this faith good works are done. Muslims are saved by their deeds and actions alone. Grace is an unmerited gift from God and is the cornerstone of Christianity. This grace is available to ALL who believe in Jesus' death, burial, and resurrection. Islam teaches the importance of righteous deeds and adherence to religious laws to attain divine approval. Even with all the good deeds, Allah makes the ultimate decision on judgment day and can do what he wills - no matter the number of good works.

It becomes clear that grace offers believers a unique sense of security and hope. The assurance that salvation is not based on human efforts but on God's unwavering love creates a profound trust in divine mercy. Faith acts as the conduit through which believers receive grace.

Paul advocates justification by faith alone—apart from the Law. James argues that genuine faith is demonstrated through works. This theological tension illustrates that while faith initiates the believer's journey, good deeds naturally flow from a transformed heart. Neither concept stands in isolation; instead, they provide a comprehensive view of a committed and visible Christian life.

Many misunderstandings about Christian salvation stem from the concept of grace. Muslims argue that grace leads to moral laxity. However, biblical teachings stress accountability even under grace. Believers are called to live responsibly and align their actions with God's teachings.

Good works, enabled by grace, become evidence of genuine faith. This showcases transformation rather than acting as a means to earn salvation. Grace also empowers believers to fulfill their divine purpose, promoting spiritual growth, and perseverance amid challenges.

Understanding the differences between grace-based (Christianity) and works-based (Islam) affects dialogue, personal faith journeys, and ethical living. Recognizing grace's role in salvation reshapes how Christians perceive their responsibilities. Additionally, appreciating the balance between faith and works fosters a more holistic approach to Christian life.

The broader consequences of these theological perspectives are significant. For Christians, embracing grace nurtures humility, gratitude, and a stronger reliance on God's mercy. It encourages living righteously out of thankfulness rather than obligation. Grace promotes genuine transformation.

It is essential to reflect on how these concepts of grace, faith, and works interplay in your spiritual journey. The call to integrate belief with action remains a central theme. You should continuously seek alignment with your faith through both conviction and practice.

Reflection

How does the concept of grace as an unearned gift from God challenge or reinforce your understanding of salvation?

How do you reconcile the teachings of Paul and James regarding faith and works?

Reflecting on Jesus' interactions with sinners and outcasts, how do you see grace's role in modern Christian outreach and ministry?

How do you respond to the Muslim perspective that good deeds are essential for salvation?

How can you demonstrate grace's transformative power in their relationships and communities?

How do you understand the balance between faith, grace, and works in your spiritual journey?

How can Christians address misunderstandings about grace and accountability when engaging in interfaith dialogues with Muslims?

Reflect on a time in your life when you experienced God's grace. How did this experience shape your faith and actions?

Chapter 9

We are Born Pure and No Such Thing as Original Sin

"We are born pure and possess no inherent original sin." Without a doubt, this statement will need to be addressed when speaking about Christianity to a Muslim. As understood in Christian theology, the idea of original sin originates from the Biblical narrative of Adam and Eve's disobedience in the Garden of Eden (Fall of Man). This doctrine suggests that the first human beings' transgression resulted in humanity inheriting a sinful nature. However, understanding the origin of this concept and its implications necessitates an exploration of relevant biblical passages and theological arguments throughout Christian history.

Origin and Nature of Sin According to The Bible

The concept of original sin, rooted in the Biblical narrative, begins with the Fall of Man. Genesis 3 recounts how Adam and Eve's disobedience in the Garden of Eden led to their expulsion. It is here that marks the inception of sin. According to the Bible, humanity's inherited sinful nature stems from this pivotal moment when Adam and Eve ate from the forbidden tree. Their actions introduced sin into the world and established a pattern of disobedience that has since tainted human nature.

The story of the Fall is more than just an ancient tale; it illustrates profound theological implications about human nature and the need for redemption. When Adam and Eve disobeyed God, they fundamentally altered their relationship with Him. This act of defiance resulted in spiritual death and separation from God. By understanding this narrative,

Christians can better comprehend why humans are inherently flawed and need divine intervention.

Genesis 3:16-19 outlines the specific punishments for Adam and Eve. While we see the immediate repercussions of their disobedience, it also sets the stage for the ongoing struggle between humanity and sin. These passages help believers appreciate the depth of human depravity and the necessity of God's redemptive plan.

Romans 3:23 captures this condition by stating that all have sinned and fall short of the glory of God. No one is exempt from the grip of sin. Total depravity suggests that every aspect of human life is affected by sin. Individuals are incapable of achieving righteousness on their own.

According to biblical teachings, understanding the depth of human depravity reveals the urgent need for salvation. Without God's grace, humanity remains in a state of moral and spiritual corruption. This doctrine emphasizes that human efforts alone cannot overcome sin; divine intervention is essential. Understanding this, Christians can better appreciate the necessity of Christ's sacrificial work and the transformative power of God's grace.

Taking it one step further, the doctrine of total depravity also highlights humanity's reliance on God for redemption. It serves as a reminder that self-sufficiency is an illusion when overcoming sin. Romans 3:10-12 further supports this idea.

"As it is written: "There is no righteous person, not even one; There is no one who understands, There is no one who seeks out God; They have all turned aside, together they have become corrupt; There is no one who does good, There is not even one." - Romans 3:10-12

These passages collectively reinforce the belief that only through acknowledging human limitations and seeking God's help can individuals hope to attain salvation.

Redemptive history traces the redemption narrative in light of humanity's fallen state. From Genesis to Revelation, the Bible unfolds God's plan for restoring His creation. John 3:16 encapsulates this divine initiative by proclaiming God's love for the world and the gift of His Son for humanity's salvation.

The Old Testament foreshadows Christ's coming through various covenants and prophecies. We have shown in previous chapters that Jesus fulfilled over 300 prophecies! The New Testament fulfills these promises in Jesus' life, death, and resurrection. It is often stated that the New Testament is in the Old Testament concealed—the Old Testament is in the New Testament revealed.

Human Nature in Christianity and Islam

Within Islamic teachings, human nature is considered inherently good. The Quran argues that humans are born pure and have a natural inclination towards good. This belief is encapsulated in Quran 30:30: "So direct your face toward the religion, inclining to truth. [Adhere to] the fitrah of Allah upon which He has created [all] people." The concept of *fitrah* refers to the innate disposition towards goodness and righteousness that Islam believes every person possesses at birth.

This Islamic perspective suggests everyone starts life with a clean slate and an intrinsic sense of morality. It emphasizes personal responsibility and accountability for one's actions rather than attributing any inherited sinful nature to individuals. Islam teaches that sin arises primarily from one's environment and choices rather than an inherent flaw within human beings. By focusing on the purity of human nature at birth, Islam encourages believers to strive towards maintaining and nurturing their intrinsic goodness throughout their lives.

Christianity offers a fundamentally different view through its doctrine of original sin. Christianity asserts that all humans inherit a sinful nature due to the Fall of Adam, the first human, as described in the Bible. Romans 5:12 states, "Therefore, just as through one man sin entered into the world, and death through sin, and so death spread to all mankind, because all sinned." This verse underpins the belief that humanity is born into sin and inherently separated from God due to the transgression of Adam. The notion of original sin implies that all humans are born predisposed to sinfulness. This necessitates a divine intervention for redemption.

The theological significance of original sin in Christianity cannot be overstated. It forms the basis for the need for salvation and the role of Jesus Christ as the redeemer. The sacrifice of Jesus on the cross serves as the means through which humanity can overcome its inherited sinful nature and attain reconciliation with God. This doctrine emphasizes the necessity of grace and faith in achieving salvation. Head over to Chapters Six, Seven, and Eight for a deeper dive and understanding of grace, faith, and salvation.

Necessity of Original Sin for Redemption

The Doctrine of Atonement directly ties original sin to the need for Christ's redemptive work. According to Ephesians 1:7, "In Him we have redemption through His blood, the forgiveness of our wrongdoings, according to the riches of His grace..." This passage states that redemption is made possible only through the atoning blood of Jesus Christ. By linking original sin with redemption, it becomes evident that, without the inherited sinful condition, the necessity of Christ's intervention and sacrifice might be questioned.

Atonement is essential because it addresses the inherent corruption introduced by original sin. Humanity's flawed nature renders individuals incapable of achieving righteousness through their efforts. Christ's atonement is necessary as it provides the only means for restoring humanity's broken relationship with God. This aligns with the overarching biblical narrative of the need for divine intervention to rectify the Fall brought about by Adam's disobedience.

Scriptural analysis supports the view that original sin necessitates the redemptive work of Christ. Expanding on Romans 5:12-19, the passage draws a parallel between Adam's transgression and Jesus' act of righteousness.

"Therefore, just as through one man sin entered into the world, and death through sin, and so death spread to all mankind, because all sinned - for until the Law sin was in the world, but sin is not counted against *anyone* when there is no law. Nevertheless death reigned from Adam until Moses, even over those who had not sinned in the likeness of the violation *committed* by Adam, who is a type of Him who was to come.

But the gracious gift is not like the offense. For if by the offense of the one the many died, much more did the grace of God and the gift by the grace of the one Man, Jesus Christ, overflow to the many. The gift is not like *that which came* through the one who sinned; for on the one hand the judgment *arose* from one *offense* , resulting in condemnation, but on the other hand the gracious gift *arose* from many offenses, resulting in justification. For if by the offense of the one, death reigned through the one, much more will those who receive the abundance of grace and of the gift of righteousness reign in life through the One, Jesus Christ.

So then, as through one offense the result was condemnation to all mankind, so also through one act of righteousness the result was justification of life to all mankind. For as through the one man's disobedience the many were made sinners, so also through the obedience of the One the many will be made righteous." - Romans 5:12-19

The passage shows how one man's sin led to condemnation for all - while another man's obedience offers justification and life. Verse 17 reinforces the connection between original sin, human depravity, and the abundant grace available through Jesus.

As discussed in the previous chapter, grace is paramount because human beings are inherently sinful and incapable of restoring themselves to a state of righteousness through their actions alone. The pervasive nature of sin, inherited from Adam, necessitates an external intervention—God's grace—to facilitate salvation. This demonstrates humanity's dependency on God's benevolence and the insufficiency of human effort in attaining redemption.

Biblical Support for Humanity's Inherent Sinfulness

Psalm 51:5 states, "Behold, I was brought forth in guilt, And in sin my mother conceived me." This passage suggests that sin is ingrained in human nature from birth. King David, the author of this Psalm, acknowledges his sinful nature from the moment of his conception. He indicates that sin is not merely an act but a condition inherited by all humans. This verse has been foundational in Christian theology, arguing that humanity is inherently sinful.

Ephesians 2:3 describes people as "by nature children of wrath." This infers that human beings are born into a state of sinfulness and deserve divine judgment. Establishing such an understanding makes it evident that sin permeates human existence from birth. The universality of sin as intrinsic to human nature provides a theological basis for understanding why redemption is necessary through Jesus Christ.

Genesis 8:21 states, "The intent of man's heart is evil from his youth." The verse reflects on the corrupt nature of humanity right from its inception. This repetitive emphasis across different scriptural texts builds a cohesive argument that sin is woven into the fabric of human existence.

Romans 3:10-11 articulates, "There is no righteous person, not even one; There is no one who understands, There is no one who seeks out God." This passage asserts that no person is inherently righteous. Human beings lack the natural inclination or understanding to seek God.

Scriptural teachings weave a consistent narrative regarding humanity's sinful nature. By compiling these scriptural foundations, believers are guided to understand the pervasive impact of sin and the importance of seeking redemption. These scriptures do not merely point out individual shortcomings; they describe a fundamental condition affecting humanity. This realization directs believers toward recognizing their dependence on God's grace and inspires a pursuit of redemption through faith.

Mitchell Beecher

Summary

Christians must understand how humanity's sinful nature originated from Adam and Eve's disobedience in the Garden of Eden. The Fall was a pivotal moment that not only introduced sin into the world but also established a pattern of disobedience that affected all humanity.

The narrative of the Fall is much more than an ancient story; it reveals profound theological truths about human nature and the need for redemption. By examining passages like Genesis 3:16-19 and Romans 3:23, we can grasp the severity of sin and its consequences on humanity. These scriptures emphasize that every aspect of human life is influenced by sin, highlighting our need for divine intervention.

Understanding human depravity according to biblical teachings shows why salvation is urgent. Without God's grace, humanity remains in a state of moral and spiritual corruption. The doctrine of total depravity states that human efforts alone are insufficient for overcoming sin. Only through Christ's sacrificial work and God's transformative grace can individuals hope to attain righteousness.

Islam teaches that humans are born pure with an innate inclination towards good. Christianity asserts that all humans inherit a sinful nature due to the Fall. These two fundamental differences influence the theological frameworks of both religions and shape beliefs and practices around morality, accountability, and redemption.

As we continue our Christian journey, we must acknowledge our dependence on divine grace and strive toward spiritual renewal. Understanding the depth of human fallenness and the provision of God's redemptive plan offers a foundation for engaging in meaningful apologetics discussions and supporting our spiritual growth.

Reflection

How do you personally understand the concept of original sin, and how has this understanding influenced your view of human nature and salvation?

In what ways does the narrative of the Fall in Genesis 3 shape your perspective on human disobedience and its consequences?'

How do Romans 3:23 and Romans 5:12-19 teachings about human sinfulness and grace resonate with your personal faith journey?

What are your thoughts on the differences between the Christian and Islamic views of human nature? How do these differences impact conversations?

How does the doctrine of total depravity influence your understanding of human effort versus divine intervention in achieving righteousness?

In light of the biblical teachings on human sinfulness, how do you see the role of grace and redemption in everyday Christian life?

Reflecting on Psalm 51:5 and Ephesians 2:3, how do these verses shape your understanding of sin being an inherent part of human nature from birth?

How do you reconcile the idea of humanity's inherent sinfulness with the belief in human potential for goodness and moral behavior?

How does the necessity of Christ's atonement for original sin deepen your appreciation for the significance of Jesus' sacrificial work on the cross?

Chapter 10

Muhammad is Mentioned in The Bible

In this final chapter, we explore the intriguing claim that Muhammad is mentioned in the Bible. By comparing interpretations held by Muslims and Christians, we will examine passages such as Deuteronomy 18:18 and Isaiah 42:1-4. These passages, among others, are frequently argued to prophesy Muhammad's coming. By carefully investigating Old and New Testament texts, including verses from the Gospel of John, we will assess the traditional Christian view that these prophecies refer to Jesus Christ or the Holy Spirit and not another prophet. This chapter navigates these claims' historical and textual contexts, highlighting how differing interpretations can challenge and enrich your dialogues.

Commonly Cited Biblical References

We begin with a close look at commonly cited verses often interpreted as prophetic references to Muhammad. One prominent verse is Deuteronomy 18:18, where God tells Moses, "I will raise up for them a prophet from among their countrymen like you, and I will put My words in his mouth, and he shall speak to them everything that I command him." Muslims argue that this refers to Muhammad. They note the parallels between Moses and Muhammad's leadership roles and various revelations. However, traditional Christian interpretation sees this prophecy fulfilled in Jesus Christ due to his Jewish lineage and fulfillment of over 300 other Old Testament prophecies.

Another significant verse is Isaiah 42:1-4. Isaiah, a prophet, speaks of a servant chosen by God who will bring justice to the nations.

"Behold, My Servant, whom I uphold; My chosen one *in whom* My soul delights. I have put My Spirit upon Him; He will bring forth justice to the nations. He will not cry out nor raise *His voice* , Nor make His voice heard in the street. A bent reed He will not break *off* And a dimly burning wick He will not extinguish; He will faithfully bring forth justice. He will not be disheartened or crushed Until He has established justice on the earth; And the coastlands will wait expectantly for His law." - Isaiah 42:1-4

This passage is sometimes linked to Muhammad due to his role in spreading Islam and establishing laws. Yet, Christian exegesis identifies this servant as Jesus and connects it to His characteristics (e.g., humility and suffering). The broader context of Isaiah further reinforces this association with the Messiah (Jesus Christ) by highlighting themes of redemption and salvation.

In the New Testament, John 1:15 mentions John the Baptist testifying about someone coming after him who is greater than he is.

"John testified about Him and called out, saying, "This was He of whom I said, 'He who is coming after me has proved to be my superior, because He existed before me.'" - John 1:15

Muslims interpret this as a reference to Muhammad and consider John's role as a precursor to a greater prophet. Nevertheless, the Christian perspective views this as referring to Jesus, whom John explicitly identified as the "Lamb of God" (John 1:29). The immediate and surrounding texts point to Jesus as central to John's ministry and testimony.

John 14:16-17, John 16:7-8, and John 16:12-13 are also frequently cited in discussions about Muhammad's potential mention in the Bible. In these verses, Jesus promises the coming of the *advocate* or *comforter* , which Muslims believe is Muhammad. Muslims argue that the description of the advocate's role aligns with Muhammad's mission to guide people. However, Christian theology clearly interprets the *advocate* as the Holy Spirit. The Holy Spirit was given to believers after Jesus' ascension. The context of Jesus' farewell discourse to his disciples supports this interpretation.

Taking John 14:16-17 logically, it does not make sense that it can be Muhammad. Jesus says, " *But* you know Him because He remains with you and will be in you." This indicates that the disciples already knew the Holy Spirit, the Holy Spirit was there, and the Holy Spirit was in them. This cannot be applied to Muhammad.

Before moving on, we need to look at one more important thing. The historical and textual contexts of these verses require a more comprehensive understanding. Deuteronomy was written within the context of Mosaic Law and its prophetic traditions. It was aimed at guiding the Israelites. Its language reflects the concerns and expectations of ancient Israelite society.

Similarly, Isaiah's prophecies emerged during periods of turmoil and exile. Isaiah offered hope and the future restoration to Israel. Understanding these historical backgrounds helps clarify why Christians see these texts as pointing to Jesus rather than another prophet.

The Gospel of John, written in the first century AD, presents a theological narrative that centers on Jesus' identity as the Son of God (see Chapter Four). John's emphasis on Jesus' divine nature and mission shapes the interpretation of its passages. Recognizing the early Christian community's struggles and the need to affirm Jesus' messianic role explains why these references fit within the Christian framework.

Problems with Misinterpretations

Discussing the implications of these misinterpretations is crucial. Misreading these biblical texts leads to misunderstandings between our Muslim friends and fosters tension instead of mutual respect. When Muslims assert that Muhammad is prophesied in the Bible, and Christians strongly disagree, usually it creates barriers to constructive dialogue. These conversations require sensitivity and a willingness to understand differing perspectives without compromising one's beliefs.

Such misinterpretations also influence how each faith perceives the other's scriptures and teachings. For instance, seeing Muhammad in the Bible could suggest to Muslims that Christianity has inherent recognition of Islam's truth claims. Christians feel their scriptures are being taken to fit the Islamic narrative. To mitigate these issues, it is essential to approach discussions focusing on shared values and respectful disagreement.

The importance of accurately interpreting biblical prophecies cannot be overstated. Accurate interpretation ensures that the original message and intent of the scripture are honored. It prevents the imposition of external meanings that might distort the text's true significance. In the context of Muhammad's alleged mentions, accuracy involves thorough explanation and a commitment to understanding the cultural and historical period in which the Bible was written.

Accurate interpretation also fosters integrity. When both parties demonstrate a commitment to truthful and respectful engagement with each other's sacred texts, it builds trust and opens avenues for deeper understanding. It allows for meaningful conversation about differences and similarities without attacks or discord.

Qualifications of Biblical Prophecy

We must examine prophecy and its meaning before addressing the passages mentioned so far. Anytime a prophecy is written, we must be able to hold it to a high standard to test the claim. The criteria that define a genuine biblical prophecy are essential to understanding the claim - especially surrounding Muhammad's alleged mentions in the Bible. An authentic biblical prophecy must meet specific qualifications. Firstly, it should come from a recognized prophet or be embedded within the accepted canon of scripture. Secondly, it often contains unambiguous language that points to future events. This distinctiveness sets it apart from general statements or teachings. For instance, prophecies predicting the Messiah in the Old Testament are precise, detailing lineage, place of birth, and significant life events. These two criteria ensure their recognition as divine predictions.

Applying these criteria to alleged prophecies regarding Muhammad necessitates careful scrutiny. It requires identifying texts purportedly referring to Muhammad and examining whether these references meet the stringent qualifications of a biblical prophecy. Deuteronomy 18:18 Moses speaks of God raising a countryman (brethren) "like you." To determine if this indeed refers to Muhammad, we must assess the specificity and clarity of the prophecy. The text must clearly outline characteristics or events corresponding to Muhammad's life and mission. Ambiguities or multiple interpretations weaken the claim and make the prophecy less robust when compared to established biblical standards.

If alleged prophecies about Muhammad fail to meet the criteria, they may be seen as speculative interpretations rather than genuine prophecies. However, if specific texts are found to align closely with Muhammad's life, it offers an opportunity for deeper mutual understanding. We must approach these discussions objectively and respect the foundational principles that govern prophetic validation in the Bible.

Examples of recognized prophetic fulfillments from biblical narratives help illustrate how specific and verifiable accurate prophecies are. For instance, the prophets Isaiah and Micah accurately foretold the birth of Jesus Christ, specifying his lineage and birthplace. Isaiah 7:14 mentions a virgin giving birth to Immanuel.

"Therefore the Lord Himself will give you a sign: Behold, the virgin will conceive and give birth to a son, and she will name Him Immanuel." - Isaiah 7:14

Micah 5:2 pinpointed Bethlehem as the Messiah's birthplace:

"But as for you, Bethlehem Ephrathah, *Too* little to be among the clans of Judah, From you One will come forth for Me to be ruler in Israel. His times of coming forth are from long ago, From the days of eternity." - Micah 5:2

These prophecies were fulfilled centuries later, as documented in the New Testament. These two example prophecies display the high standard of clarity and detail expected in biblical prophecies. Such precedents set a benchmark against which other claims, including those about Muhammad, must be measured.

Biblical prophecies typically offer more detailed and contextually aligned descriptions, leaving little room for alternative interpretations. For instance, Muhammad's mentioned role in historical texts often hinges on broader and less definitive terms. These distinctions provide a clearer understanding of what constitutes a prophecy and help prevent misapplications of prophetic standards. We must focus on maintaining theological coherence while respecting Islamic traditions and interpretations.

Clear and specific Biblical prophecies stand firm against skepticism and form a vital part of the Christian faith and history. They demonstrate divine foresight and strengthen believers' convictions by fulfilling expectations precisely as written. Ambiguous or vague prophecies, however, risk being dismissed as coincidental or retrofitted interpretations. Clarity and specificity are critical markers of valid and relevant prophecies.

These markers play a pivotal role when discussing alleged prophecies about Muhammad. Passages from the Bible claimed to refer to Muhammad must demonstrate clarity and specificity comparable to well-established prophecies. These elements are necessary for such claims to succeed under critical examination. Therefore, engaging with these texts demands rigorous analysis and an honest evaluation of their prophetic credentials. This approach

Mitchell Beecher

ensures that conclusions are based on sound scriptural principles rather than interpretative biases or assumptions.

Addressing Misinterpretations and Confirming Christ-Centric Prophecies

Let us go back to the passages commonly debated around Muhammad's predictions—John 14:16-17, John 16:7-8, and John 16:12-13. These verses refer to the *comforter* or *advocate* . Christians understand this to be the Holy Spirit. The Greek word is *Parakletos* —meaning intercessor, consoler, advocate, comforter. Muslims unequivocally believe that this is a prophecy for Muhammad. However, this interpretation fails to align with the broader scriptural context.

Deuteronomy 18:18 is the other verse used. This verse states, "I will raise up for them a prophet from among their countrymen like you, and I will put My words in his mouth, and he shall speak to them everything that I command him." Some translations translate the Greek *countrymen* as *brethren* " - אָח)*ach* "). Muslims argue that this prophecy refers to Muhammad. They point out similarities, such as both being lawgivers and leading large communities. They also note that "countrymen" refer to the Ishmaelites. This makes Muhammad a plausible candidate since he was an Arab (descendant of Ishmael).

Moses delivered this prophecy to the Israelites during their journey through the wilderness. He emphasized God's commitment to guide them through future prophets. A pivotal point to consider is that *countrymen* commonly refer to fellow Israelites in the Old Testament. Interpreting *countrymen* as referring to the descendants of Ishmael rather than the Israelites themselves is less consistent with the broader usage of the term in the scripture. Moses' immediate audience was the Israelites and not the Ishmaelites. Moses clearly stated that the prophet would be from among their own people.

Several Christian interpretations suggest that Jesus Christ fulfills this prophecy more fittingly. The New Testament frequently cites Jesus as performing roles

118

strikingly similar to those of Moses. An example is being a mediator between God and humanity. Jesus perfectly fits the description of a prophet who directly communicates God's will to humanity. Consequently, while Muhammad may share some characteristics with Moses, the deeper textual and cultural analysis of Deuteronomy 18:18 aligns more closely with Jesus.

Reviewing the surrounding chapters and other prophetic writings within the Bible is helpful. Doing so reveals that the Israelites sought a mediator to convey God's words directly to them - "Then they said to Moses, "Speak to us yourself and we will listen; but do not have God speak to us, or we will die!" (Exodus 20:19) This comes following their fear of hearing His voice at Mount Horeb. Moses relayed God's assurance that a new prophet would fulfill this role and offered comfort and guidance.

Contextual analysis shows that the prophet mentioned in Deuteronomy is expected to arise among the Israelite community. This alone complicates the notion that Muhammad is the subject of this prophecy. Further examination of the qualities attributed to Jesus in the New Testament supports the idea that he embodies the foretold figure in Deuteronomy more appropriately.

One must apply exegetical principles that consider historical, cultural, and linguistic contexts to correct these errors. Understanding the Greek term *Parakletos* in John's Gospel highlights its connotations of comfort and advocacy. These characteristic roles are attributed to the Holy Spirit and not Muhammad. A simple examination of Muhammad's life and behavior shows that - stoned a woman for adultery (Hussaini, S. (2009), killed those who insulted him (Bukhari 4:241. (n.d.)), consummated a married with nine year old (Hussaini, S. (2009a), etc. Examining the Hebrew phraseology and audience in Deuteronomy clarifies it addresses Israelite succession and not any external figures. By contextualizing these verses, one aligns interpretations of Christianity, not Islam.

Summary

The continuity between the Old and New Testaments consistently centers on God's relationship with Israel and the anticipated Messiah. Jesus Christ fulfills the thematic threads of messianic prophecy. Maintaining theological coherence in interpreting biblical texts cannot be stressed enough. When evaluating alleged Biblical prophetic references to Muhammad, it is crucial to adhere to principles that preserve the integrity of scripture. This involves respecting each biblical book's genre, purpose, and context.

Old and New Testament prophecies clearly point to someone other than Muhammad. The Old Testament prophecies point to a Messiah—someone who will rescue and save humanity from death's grip. Jesus, in the New Testament, clearly says He will send an *advocate* to help guide and comfort us. This *advocate* will live inside us.

When evaluating claims about Muhammad in the Bible, we must adhere to the consistency of key Christian beliefs - the Trinity, the incarnation, and salvation through Christ alone. Any interpretation suggesting a prophetic role for Muhammad must be scrutinized against these fundamental doctrines. If such interpretations compromise the coherent teaching of scripture, they should not be considered Biblical prophecies.

As you continue to investigate the claim of Muhammad in the Bible and the other nine objections mentioned in this book, I'll leave you with some practical guidance:

- Adopt a humble and prayerful approach to studying scripture.

- Engage with historical and contemporary theological scholarship (e.g., Bible commentaries).

- Lean on your church community when questions need answering.

These simple actions will not only help clear up any misinformation but will also help foster understanding and respect when dialoguing with Muslims.

Jesus lived and died to offer hope and a better life to all people, regardless of race, nationality, past actions, or religious upbringing, promising a brighter future on earth and beyond.

Reflection

How do you interpret Deuteronomy 18:18 in the context of the broader narrative of the Old Testament? Do you see it pointing to Jesus, Muhammad, or another figure? Why?

Isaiah 42:1-4 speaks of a servant bringing justice to the nations. How do you see this prophecy being fulfilled? What qualities or actions align more closely with Jesus or Muhammad?

When discussing the role of John the Baptist in John 1:15, how does the context influence your understanding of whom he was referring to? What are the key elements that lead you to your conclusion?

The *comforter* or *advocate* in John 14:16-17, 16:7-8, and 16:12-13 is significant in Christian theology. How do you differentiate between the Holy Spirit and Muhammad in these passages? What evidence supports your view?

Consider the historical and cultural contexts of Deuteronomy and Isaiah. How do these contexts influence your interpretation of the prophecies? Are these contexts essential in understanding the true meaning of these texts?

How do you approach the concept of biblical prophecy? What criteria do you use to determine whether a prophecy is genuine?

How do the specific and verifiable prophecies about Jesus in the Old Testament, such as Isaiah 7:14 and Micah 5:2, influence your understanding of what constitutes a genuine prophecy?

How can you ensure that your interpretations of biblical prophecies remain consistent with the key doctrines of your faith?

Conclusion

Throughout this book, we dove deep into crucial topics and objections commonly raised by Muslims and offer clear biblical responses to each challenge. Let's briefly recap the key points:

1. **The Bible is Corrupted:** We examined the historical and textual evidence that supports the reliability of the Bible and affirms its divine inspiration (2 Timothy 3:16-17).

2. **There are Many Different Bibles and Versions:** We clarified the differences between translations and demonstrated that the core message of the Bible remains unchanged (Isaiah 40:8).

3. **Jesus is Not God and Never Claimed to Be:** We explored the numerous biblical passages in which Jesus unequivocally claims divinity, such as John 10:30 and John 8:58.

4. **God Cannot Have a Son:** We discussed the unique relationship between God the Father and Jesus the Son and emphasized how the Bible lays the foundation of the Sonship of Christ (John 3:16).

5. **Trinity Means Three Gods:** We explained the doctrine of the Trinity - showing that it represents one God in three persons and not three separate gods (Matthew 28:19).

6. **Jesus was Not Crucified and Atonement is Not Necessary:** We provided evidence for the historical crucifixion of Jesus and explained the necessity of atonement for the forgiveness of sins (1 Corinthians 15:3-4).

7. **God Would not Let a Prophet like Jesus Suffer the Disgrace of the Cross:** We discussed the prophetic

significance and the purpose behind Jesus' suffering and crucifixion (Isaiah 53:5).

8. **Saved by Deeds and Not by Grace:** We reaffirmed the biblical teaching that salvation is by grace through faith and not by works (Ephesians 2:8-9).

9. **We are Born Pure and No Such Thing as Original Sin:** We examined the doctrine of original sin and its implications, showing that all have sinned and fall short of God's glory (Romans 3:23).

10. **Muhammad is Mentioned in The Bible:** We reviewed the claims that Muhammad is prophesied in the Bible and demonstrated that these interpretations do not align with the biblical context (John 14:16).

Take a moment to consider how your perspective on key beliefs in Christianity and Islam has evolved as you engaged with the biblical foundations presented in response to Islamic objections. This journey has been about addressing challenges and deepening our understanding of the Christian faith. Reflect on how your knowledge has grown and how these insights can shape your conversations and relationships with others.

Consider how you can incorporate the knowledge acquired from this book into meaningful conversations with Muslims that foster mutual understanding and respect for our differing beliefs. Use these chapters' biblical responses and perspectives to engage in thoughtful, compassionate, and respectful dialogue. Remember, the goal is not to win arguments but to share the truth in love (Ephesians 4:15) and to build bridges of understanding.

Let this book be the starting point of a journey towards greater understanding. Challenge yourself to engage in constructive discussions and seek opportunities for mutual growth in knowledge and faith. Continue to study the Bible diligently, pray for wisdom, and seek the guidance of the Holy Spirit in all your interactions. Let us be ambassadors for Christ and share His love and truth with a world that desperately needs both (2 Corinthians 5:20).

As you go forward, may you be inspired to live out your faith boldly, equipped with the knowledge, and understand the need to respond to objections with grace and truth. May your conversations be filled with the Holy Spirit and compassion. May your faith be strengthened and your love for Jesus shine brightly in all you do.

List of References

Chapter 1
Are Biblical Manuscripts Reliable?. C.S. Lewis Institute. (n.d.). https://www.cslewisinstitute.org/resources/are-biblical-manuscripts-reliable/
Biblical Manuscripts | Houston Christian University. hc.edu. (2019, October). https://hc.edu/museums/dunham-bible-museum/tour-of-the-museum/past-exhibits/biblical-manuscripts/
Bird, M. (2018, September). The Reliability of the New Testament, Part 2: Internal and External Evidence Tests. Holy Joys. https://holyjoys.org/the-reliability-of-the-new-testament-part-2-internal-and-external-evidence-tests/
Inspiration, Preservation, and New Testament Textual Criticism | Bible.org. bible.org. (n.d.). https://bible.org/article/inspiration-preservation-and-new-testament-textual-criticism
Manuscript Support for the Bible's Relia. Reasoning From The S. (n.d.). https://www.ronrhodes.org/manuscript-support-for-the-bible-s-relia
Slick, M. (2008, December). Manuscript evidence for superior New Testament reliability. Christian Apologetics & Research Ministry. https://carm.org/about-the-bible/manuscript-evidence-for-superior-new-testament-reliability/
Textual Reliability of the New Testament. www.tektonics.org. (n.d.). https://www.tektonics.org/lp/nttextcrit.php

Chapter 2
"As Far as It Is Translated Correctly": Bible Translation and the Church | Religious Studies Center. rsc.byu.edu. (n.d.). https://rsc.byu.edu/vol-20-no-2-2019/far-it-translated-correctly-bible-translation-church

Faith, E., Titus 2:3-5, S. (n.d.). Bible translations: Comparison charts. Chapter 3 Ministries. https://www.chapter3min.org/bible-translations-comparison-charts/

How Our Cultural Context Impacts the Way We Interpret Scripture | faithward.org. faithward.org. (2022, January). https://www.faithward.org/understanding-the-bible/how-our-cultural-context-impacts-the-way-we-interpret-scripture/

How We Got the Bible. bible.org. (n.d.). https://bible.org/book/export/html/6419

webmaster. (2022, July). Bible Translation is the Key to a Christian Faith "at Home" in Any Culture - Missio Nexus. Missio Nexus. https://missionexus.org/bible-translation-is-the-key-to-a-christian-faith-at-home-in-any-culture%ef%bf%bc/

Chapter 3

Council of Nicea. Christian History Institute. (n.d.). https://christianhistoryinstitute.org/study/module/nicea

Ford, C. (2020, April). Christological Controversies in the Early Church. The Gospel Coalition. https://www.thegospelcoalition.org/essay/christological-controversies-in-the-early-church/

Letham, R. (n.d.). The Deity of Christ. The Gospel Coalition. https://www.thegospelcoalition.org/essay/the-deity-of-christ/

Schrock, D. (n.d.). Jesus as the Son of God. The Gospel Coalition. https://www.thegospelcoalition.org/essay/jesus-as-the-son-of-god/

Stamps, L. (2023). The Humanity of Christ. The Gospel Coalition. https://www.thegospelcoalition.org/essay/the-humanity-of-christ/

Chapter 4

Clark, E. (n.d.). Love Muslims. Proclaim Jesus Is 'Son of God.'. The Gospel Coalition. https://www.thegospelcoalition.org/article/jesus-son-god/

Emery, G. (2021, January). The Best Guide for Understanding the Trinity. Church Life Journal. https://

churchlifejournal.nd.edu/articles/the-best-guide-for-understanding-the-trinity/

Father and Son - The Relationship Between Jesus And God. The Oneness Of God In Christ. (n.d.). https://www.theonenessofgod.org/father-and-son-the-relationship-between-jesus-and-god/

Jesus and the Father. Desiring God. (2005, February). https://www.desiringgod.org/messages/jesus-and-the-father

Misconceptions Clarified X; "Who Were The Sons Of God?". Road2TheCross. (2017, March). https://www.road2thecross.org/truth-blog/2017/3/5/misconceptions-clarified-x-who-were-the-sons-of-god

Thornton, C. (n.d.). The Trinity | TGC Essays | Christine Thornton. The Gospel Coalition. https://www.thegospelcoalition.org/essay/the-trinity/

Was Jesus (as) Really the 'Son of God'? - Examining the Historical Context. The Review of Religions. (2021, December). https://www.reviewofreligions.org/35615/was-jesus-as-really-the-son-of-god-examining-the-historical-context/

Why Muslims Are Repelled by the Term Son of God | Missio Nexus. missionexus.org. (n.d.). https://missionexus.org/why-muslims-are-repelled-by-the-term-son-of-god/

Chapter 5

Answering Muslim Objections to the Trinity.
www.answering-islam.org

. (n.d.). https://www.answering-islam.org/authors/hartman/trinity_objections.html

Five Major Problems with the Trinity - Restitutio. restitutio.org. (n.d.). https://restitutio.org/2019/01/19/five-major-problems-with-the-trinity/

Perman, M. (2006, January). What Is the Doctrine of the Trinity?. Desiring God. https://www.desiringgod.org/articles/what-is-the-doctrine-of-the-trinity

Sica, C. (2019, July). St. Augustine's Analogy for Understanding the Trinity. mcgrathblog.nd.edu. https://

mcgrathblog.nd.edu/st.-augustines-analogy-for-understanding-the-trinity

Staff, P. (2015, August). The best analogy for the Trinity (hold your stones) -. The Project on Lived Theology. https://www.livedtheology.org/best-analogy-trinity-hold-stones/

TGC Course | The Doctrine of the Trinity. The Gospel Coalition. (n.d.). https://www.thegospelcoalition.org/course/the-doctrine-of-the-trinity/

The Doctrine of the Trinity at Nicaea and Chalcedon. www.str.org.

(n.d.). https://www.str.org/w/the-doctrine-of-the-trinity-at-nicaea-and-chalcedon

Chapter 6

Answering 4 Common Objections to Penal Substitutionary Atonement. 9Marks. (n.d.). https://www.9marks.org/article/answering-4-common-objections-to-psa/

Evidence for the historical existence of Jesus Christ - RationalWiki. Rationalwiki.org. (2004). https://rationalwiki.org/wiki/Evidence_for_the_historical_existence_of_Jesus_Christ

Harrington, B. (2019, April). The Historical Evidence for the Death, Burial and Resurrection of Jesus - Evidence for Easter Part 3. Renew. https://renew.org/the-historical-evidence-for-the-death-burial-and-resurrection-of-jesus-evidence-for-easter-part-3/

Morrison, S. (2014, October). 7 Theories of the Atonement Summarized. Stephen D. Morrison. https://www.sdmorrison.org/7-theories-of-the-atonement-summarized/

Philosophical Objections to the Atonement | Reasonable Faith. www.reasonablefaith.org.

(n.d.). https://www.reasonablefaith.org/media/reasonable-faith-podcast/philosophical-objections-to-the-atonement/

The Christian Doctrine of Substitutionary Atonement | Dwell Community Church. Dwell Community Church. (n.d.).

https://www.dwellcc.org/essays/christian-doctrine-substitutionary-atonement

Thurow, J. (2023, April). Atonement. plato.stanford.edu. https://plato.stanford.edu/Entries/atonement/

Chapter 7

An Explanation of Divine Sacrifice – LarrySanger.org. * (2020, February). https://larrysanger.org/2020/02/divine-sacrifice/

Axton, A. (2019, August). The Lie of the Divine Necessity of Sacrifice Exposed by Christ. Forging Ploughshares. https://forgingploughshares.org/2019/08/29/the-lie-of-the-divine-necessity-of-sacrifice-exposed-by-christ/

Godfrey, N. (2014, April). Jesus' Crucifixion As Symbol of Destruction of Temple and Judgment on the Jews. Vridar. https://vridar.org/2014/04/18/jesus-crucifixion-as-symbol-of-destruction-of-temple-and-judgment-on-the-jews/

Huijgen, A. (n.d.). The Theology of the Canons of Dort: A Reassessment After Four Hundred Years. CURRENT DEBATES IN REFORMED THEOLOGY: PRACTICE. https://www.academia.edu/55867700/The_Theology_of_the_Canons_of_Dort_A_Reassessment_After_Four_Hundred_Years

Sermons | Fellowship Bible Church of Ann Arbor. www.fbcaa.org. (n.d.). https://www.fbcaa.org/Sermons

The Psychology of Crucifixion. www.1517.org. (n.d.). https://www.1517.org/articles/the-psychology-of-crucifixion

Wayne, L. (2021, November). What was the Crucifixion?. Christian Apologetics & Research Ministry. https://carm.org/about-jesus/what-was-the-crucifixion/

Chapter 8

Cobabe, G. (2008, January). Salvation by Works or Salvation by Grace - Who Really Believes What?. FAIR.

https://www.fairlatterdaysaints.org/blog/2008/01/11/salvation-by-works-or-salvation-by-grace-who-really-beleive-what
Ephesians 5:15-16 Commentary | Precept Austin. www.preceptaustin.org.
(n.d.). https://www.preceptaustin.org/ephesians_515-16

God, U. (2019, September). Grace in Action: Jesus Christ's Example. United Church of God. https://www.ucg.org/bible-study-tools/bible-study-aids/what-does-the-bible-teach-about-grace/grace-in-action-jesus-christs-example

K. C. Moser: The Way of Salvation: Chapter 4: Repentance And Faith. webfiles.acu.edu. (n.d.). https://webfiles.acu.edu/departments/Library/HR/restmov_nov11/www.mun.ca/rels/restmov/texts/moser/chap4.html

Misinterpreting Common Grace. Countryside Bible Church. (n.d.). https://countrysidebible.org/sermons/20150315a-110866

OFM, F. (2022, September). Daily Meditation: The Power of Forgiveness. Center for Action and Contemplation. https://cac.org/daily-meditations/the-power-of-forgiveness-2022-09-16/

Philippians 2:1-2 Commentary | Precept Austin. www.preceptaustin.org.
(n.d.). https://www.preceptaustin.org/philippians_21-4

Storms, S. (n.d.). Saving Grace. The Gospel Coalition. https://www.thegospelcoalition.org/essay/saving-grace/

Chapter 9

Christ Covenant Church. (2022, February). 4 Differences Between Christianity & Islam. Christ Covenant Church: Knoxville, TN. https://www.christcov.org/seths-soundbites/post/4-differences-between-christianity-islam

Concept of God in Islam and Christianity | Reasonable Faith. Reasonablefaith.org. (2019). https://www.reasonablefaith.org/writings/popular-writings/christianity-other-faiths/concept-of-god-in-islam-and-christianity/

Ellis, P. (2022, August). Original Sin is Unbiblical. Escape to Reality. https://escapetoreality.org/2022/08/03/original-sin-is-unbiblical/

GotQuestions.org. (2015, January). What is the sin nature? | GotQuestions.org. GotQuestions.org. https://www.gotquestions.org/sin-nature.html

Perman, M. (2019, April). What Is the Biblical Evidence for Original Sin?. Desiring God. https://www.desiringgod.org/articles/what-is-the-biblical-evidence-for-original-sin

Phillips, R. (2024). Original Sin. The Gospel Coalition. https://www.thegospelcoalition.org/essay/original-sin/

Chapter 10

Ariarajah, S. (2015). The Bible in interfaith dialogue. Cambridge University Press. https://www.cambridge.org/core/books/new-cambridge-history-of-the-bible/bible-in-interfaith-dialogue/24778FF3C093D58095EDA5E6AD07E7F1

Biblical prophecies about Muhammad. Al Islam. (2011, November). https://www.alislam.org/articles/biblical-prophecies-about-muhammad/

Carson, D., Netland, H., Sweeney, D. (2016, March). The Message of Islam vs. The Gospel of Jesus. The Gospel Coalition. https://www.thegospelcoalition.org/article/the-message-of-islam-vs-the-gospel-of-jesus/

Finding and Following Jesus: The Muslim Claim to the Messiah. Yaqeen Institute for Islamic Research. (n.d.). https://yaqeeninstitute.org/read/paper/finding-and-following-jesus-the-muslim-claim-to-the-messiah

Hussaini, S. (2009, July 2). Sahih Muslim Book 17, Hadith Number 4206. Hadith Collection. https://hadithcollection.com/sahihmuslim/sahih-muslim-book-17-punishments-prescribed-by-islam/sahih-muslim-book-017-hadith-number-4206

Bukhari 4:241. (n.d.). https://hadith.wwpa.com/page/bukhari-4-241

Hussaini, S. (2009a, June 28). Sahih Muslim Book 8, Hadith Number 3309. Hadith Collection. https://

hadithcollection.com/sahihmuslim/sahih-muslim-book-08-marriage/sahih-muslim-book-008-hadith-number-3309

Glossary

Adhan : The call to prayer.

Alhamdulillah : "All praise be to Allah"; expression of gratitude. Islamic analogue of *hallelujah* .

Allah : The Arabic word for God.

Allahu Akbar : "Allah is the Greatest"; often used in prayers.

Aqeedah : Creed or belief system in Islam.

Assalamu Alaikum : "Peace be upon you"; Islamic greeting.

Astaghfirullah : An Arabic expression meaning "God forbid!"

Ayah : A verse in the Quran.

Bismillah : "In the name of Allah"; said before starting any task.

Dawah : The act of inviting people to Islam.

Dhikr : Remembrance of Allah through recitation.

Dua : Supplication or prayer.

Eid al-Adha : Festival commemorating the willingness of Ibrahim (Abraham) to sacrifice his son.

Eid al-Fitr : Festival marking the end of Ramadan.

Fatwa : A decision or ruling by a Muslim authority.

Fiqh : Islamic jurisprudence.

Five Pillars of Islam : The fundamental practices required by all Muslims. Creed (shahadah), prayer (salaat), month of fasting (Ramadan, or sawm), giving (zakat), and pilgrimage to Mecca and Medina (Hajj).

Hadith : An authoritative collection of stories about Muhammad's life, habits, and commands, compiled centuries later.

Hajj : The pilgrimage to Mecca, required once in a lifetime.

Halal : Permissible according to Islamic law.

Haram : Forbidden according to Islamic law.

Hijab : Modest dress for Muslim women, including a headscarf.

Iftar : The meal breaking the fast during Ramadan.

Imam : A leader of prayer in a mosque.

Insha'Allah : "If Allah wills"; expression of hope for the future.

Injeel : The Arabic name of the Gospel of Jesus; an important book Christians call the New Testament.

Isa : The Arabic name for Jesus.

Jahannam : Hell in Islam.

Jannah : Paradise or heaven in Islam.

Jihad : Struggle or effort in the way of Allah.

Jizya : A religious tax placed on non-Muslims

Jumu'ah : The Friday prayer congregation.

Ka'aba : The sacred cube-shaped structure in Mecca.

Kafir : A non-believer in Islam, infidel

Madrasa : An Islamic religious school.

Masjid : Another term for mosque, a place of worship for Muslims.

Qibla : The direction of prayer towards the Kabah in Mecca.

Quran : The holy book of Islam.

Raka'ah : A unit of prayer.

Ramadan : The ninth month of the Islamic calendar, a time of fasting.

Sadqa : Voluntary charity given by Muslims, often to prevent misfortune.

Salam : Arabic greeting meaning "peace."

Salaat : The five daily prayers in Islam.

Sawm : Fasting during the month of Ramadan.

Shahada : The Islamic declaration of faith.

Sharia : Islamic law derived from the Quran and Sunnah.

Shirk : The unforgivable sin in Islam, roughly equivalent to idolatry, placing something over the position of Allah.

Sirah : Biographical accounts of Prophet Muhammad.

Sunnah : The practices of Prophet Muhammad.

Tawhid : The concept of the oneness of Allah.

Wudhu : Ritual washing before prayers.
Zakat : Obligatory charity given by Muslims.
Zabur : the songs of David (Psalms).

Browse our collection of books, resources, apparel, and gifts at <www.timelesstruthcollection.com> .

www.ingramcontent.com/pod-product-compliance
Lightning Source LLC
Chambersburg PA
CBHW060536130626
46553CB00002B/779